Getting and Keeping the Job

SUCCESS IN BUSINESS AND TECHNICAL CAREERS

Second Edition

Val Clark

SPOKANE COMMUNITY COLLEGE

To Don Bressler who was instrumental in beginning the process.

Val Clark

Prentice Hall

Upper Saddle River, New Jersey

Columbus, Ohio

Library of Congress Cataloging-in-Publication Data

Clark, Val.
    Getting and keeping the job : success in business and technical careers / Val Clark.—
2nd ed.
      p. cm.
    Originally published: Boston : Allyn and Bacon, c1999.
    Includes bibliographical references and index.
    ISBN 0-13-061875-6
    1. Job hunting.   2. Business—Vocational guidance.   3. Industrial technicians—Vocational
guidance.   I. Title

HF5382.7 .C55 2002
650.14—dc21
                        2001053684

To Lois J. Roach, a truly courageous person. She is my mentor, inspiration, and friend.
Lois is the person who originated many of the concepts in this textbook.

Vice President and Publisher: Jeffery W. Johnston
Senior Acquisitions Editor: Sande Johnson
Assistant Editor: Cecilia Johnson
Production Editor: Holcomb Hathaway
Design Coordinator: Diane C. Lorenzo
Cover Designer: Jeff Vanik
Cover Art: Corbis/The Stock Market
Production Manager: Pamela D. Bennett
Director of Marketing: Ann Castel Davis
Director of Advertising: Kevin Flanagan
Marketing Manager: Christina Quadhamer

This book was set in Sabon by Aerocraft Charter Art Service. It was printed and bound by Banta Book Group.
The cover was printed by Phoenix Color Corp.

Pearson Education Ltd., *London*
Pearson Education Australia Pty. Limited, *Sydney*
Pearson Education Singapore Pte. Ltd.
Pearson Education North Asia Ltd., *Hong Kong*
Pearson Education Canada, Ltd., *Toronto*
Pearson Educación de Mexico, S.A. de C.V.
Pearson Education–Japan, *Tokyo*
Pearson Education Malaysia Pte. Ltd.
Pearson Education, *Upper Saddle River, New Jersey*

Prentice
Hall

10 9 8 7 6 5 4 3 2 1
ISBN 0-13-061875-6

Contents

3   Creating Interest in Yourself   67

4   What Was That You Said? Telephoning and Listening   97

5 The Interview: Preparing Well and Doing Your Best   119

6 Communicating Effectively with External Customers   153

7 Teamwork: Communicating Productively with Coworkers   169

Preface

This book details communication skills potential employees can use to be successful during the job search and to be productive once they are employed in business or technical careers. The information below is based on research conducted between July and September, 2000. This was the fourth in a series of surveys previously conducted by the author in 1984, 1993, and 1998. This most recent survey included a section asking employers about computer skills necessary for the workplace. Employers in nine states returned the latest survey. A summary of their 329 responses is listed below and included in later chapters.

Which communication skills do employers expect applicants to demonstrate *during* employment interviews for technical and business positions?

Number of respondents	329
Ability to describe their background and qualifications	217
Nonverbal communication (eye contact, handshake, etc.)	182
Ability to listen attentively	144
Ability to state personal goals clearly	114
Ability to express ideas enthusiastically	112
Other	37

What are the communication skills employees need to utilize *after* they are hired in order to be successful on the job?

Number of respondents	329
Communicating with customers effectively	254
Following directions efficiently	251
Getting along with other employees	198
Communicating in a small group productively	171
Accepting criticism non-defensively	131
Other	19

These employers were consulted to provide both job applicants and instructors with increased understanding of the communication skills employers believe are necessary for relating to coworkers and customers productively. The ideas and exercises in this book evolved from this research and the author's years of teaching students how to get a job and keep it.

This second edition includes methods for research and responding via the computer that are possible with new technology.

A brief overview of the text follows.

OVERVIEW

Chapters in this new edition include the following features:

- "World of Work": reports of actual work experiences
- "Tools of Communication": practical skill exercises
- "Stress Less" exercises
- Case studies based on real employment histories
- A project relating to specific chapter concepts
- Discussion questions to reinforce the chapter's learning objectives

The book's chapters can be broken into three groups:

Chapters 1, 2, and 3 focus on being prepared for the job search. They will help you analyze your attitudes, skills, communication styles, and work experience. You will learn to prepare and present your resume and portfolio. Techniques for researching companies, writing cover letters, and completing accurate application forms are also discussed in this first section.

Chapters 4 and 5 focus on listening proficiencies and understanding various types of employment interviews. Sample interview questions and responses are included.

Chapters 6 and 7 focus on communicating effectively with customers and coworkers. In addition, we cover the essential skills of working productively in teams and using problem-solving skills. (Many employers involved in the research and the surveys discussed earlier confirmed the need for employees to be able to work in self-managed work teams and to employ group problem-solving abilities.)

A NOTE TO STUDENTS

Read the text carefully, complete the exercises thoughtfully, and practice regularly using the skills you learn. This process will help you be better prepared to apply for a job and better equipped to succeed on the job. Complete the "Stress Less" exercises to reduce the frustrations of the job search as well as stress brought about by life, school, and job challenges.

A NOTE TO INSTRUCTORS

This material includes exercises, evaluation criteria, and feedback forms, along with practical work examples, case studies, and discussion questions. By using the various "Tools of Communication" as in-class or out-of-class assignments, you can enhance the students' skills while reducing your class preparation time. Suggested lesson plans for 12- and 16-week classes are included below.

CONSIDERATIONS FOR PREPARING LESSON PLANS

Your class content will depend on the following factors:

- The number of students enrolled in your course or workshop,

- The amount of time allotted for the class (two, three, four, or five hours per week), and
- The number of weeks the course or workshop will meet.

Consequently, you must consider many variables when planning exercises, conferences, and lectures.

SUGGESTIONS FOR LESSON PLANS

- Quarter ideas (10 or 12 weeks)
- Semester suggestions (16 weeks)
  (W) Workshops

First Topic: Assessing Attitudes and Skills
- Attitude, skills assessment (W)
- Communication style analysis (W)

Chapter 1 Project
- Employer Survey—students conduct and discuss

Second Topic: Constructing Resumes
- Resume worksheet (W)
- Evaluate resumes (W)
- Resume conferences
- Prepare an original resume and an electronic variation
- Prepare another, different type of resume

Chapter 2 Project
- Organize a portfolio

Third Topic: Selling Yourself
- Research companies (W)
  —On the Internet
  —Using other sources
- Write and evaluate cover letters (W)
  —Unsolicited
  —Solicited
- Complete application forms (W)

Chapter 3 Project
- Create a Web page
- *Extra idea*—create a CD-ROM of your Web page

Fourth Topic: Listening Efficiently
- Practice telephone employment searches with audiotapes (W)
- Practice listening skills with a log
- Practice rewording information for accuracy (W)
- Discuss barriers to communication

Chapter 4 Project

- Discuss Case Study in groups

Fifth Topic: Interviewing Effectively

■ ● Pre-interview preparation (W)

   —Checklist

   —Process

■ ● Questions (W)

   —Analysis

   —Answers

   —Asking

■ ● Interviews (W)

   —Structures

   —Types

   —Practice

     —Screening

     —Focused

■ ● Follow-up thank-you letters (W)

Chapter 5 Project

■ ● Videotape focused interviews with professional interviewers and evaluations

Sixth Topic: Relating to Customers, Externally

■ ● Learn names

■ ● Understand customers (W)

   —Needs

   —Differences in perception

   —On the telephone

   —Criticism

   —Cultural differences

Chapter 6 Project

- Sales or service presentation—verbal, written, and evaluation

Seventh Topic: Teamwork—Relating to Customers, Internally

■ ● Build a positive work climate (W)

■ ● Non-defensive communication (W)

● Giving, receiving, and evaluating instructions

● Leadership styles analysis

● Give orders effectively

■ ● Solve problems creatively in groups

Chapter 7 Project

- Organize a company and conduct group presentations

ACKNOWLEDGMENTS

During the revision of this textbook, I received great support from the staff of the Prentice Hall division of Pearson Education. I appreciated the assistance and guidance of Senior Editor Sande Johnson, Assistant Editor Cecilia Johnson, and marketing team Christina Quadhamer and Barbara Koontz. Jenine Duffy from Allyn and Bacon provided tremendous encouragement in the publishing of the first edition.

I also want to express my gratitude to those who assisted in the research process and employer survey tabulation: Tim Aman, research librarian; Leslie Miller, accounting faculty; and Chie Kuroda, student aide.

I appreciate the support of those in my office and classes who supplied their computer skills: Carmelita Brown, Shiho Matsuda, David Morgan, Julie Fechner, Yuko Asakawa, and David Hess.

This second edition especially benefited from the editorial and organizational skills of Marci McLaughlin.

I appreciated the thoughtful comments of these individuals:

Jason Archibald, instructor; Dennie Carlson, department chair, Applied Education; Sara Edlin, instructor, Applied Education; Shyamali Hauth, communication instructor; Pete O'Brien, writing instructor; Rose Poirot, writing/communication instructor; Jim Ridenour, writing/communication instructor; and Bob Wise, communication studies instructor. All of these individuals taught with and/or offered feedback on this new edition while at Spokane Community College.

Again, I want to thank my best friend, fan, and husband, Dean Clark, who has continued to be very supportive and encouraging during the writing process.

Val Clark
Spokane Community College
N. 1810 Greene St.
Spokane, WA 99217-5399

Introduction

Now you have completed most of your training and are ready to look for employment. Before knocking on employers' doors, it is usually necessary to do some additional preparation. Be prepared by:

- analyzing your personal strengths, attitudes, assets, and areas for growth.
- organizing a written sales campaign about yourself before you look for employment.
- researching companies you are interested in working for to be better equipped to ask and answer questions about these companies.
- knowing which communication skills employers expect during the job interview and on the job.
- understanding customers' needs.
- knowing how to work as a team member. Many companies, large and small, desire employees with teamwork skills.

This book is full of suggestions, ideas, and information about some of the best ways of analyzing yourself and your abilities, along with resume samples and portfolio suggestions to help you present yourself effectively. Also included are sample letters of application, methods for researching companies you want to work for, and recommendations that describe successful ways of communicating during the job interview with confidence and professionalism.

1

Analyzing Yourself and the Trends of the Job Market

LEARNING OBJECTIVES

1. Know what employers expect.

2. Understand the value of a positive attitude, and evaluate your own attitude.

3. Learn techniques for improving a neutral or negative attitude.

4. Assess your transferable job skills and analyze your previous employment experiences.

5. Learn how to analyze and use different communication styles.

6. Know the communication skills employers expect interviewees to demonstrate during job interviews.

7. Examine recent trends in the workplace.

8. Discuss the results of survey research to determine which communication and computer skills employers want job applicants to possess.

9. Apply chapter concepts through case studies, projects, and discussion questions.

Whether you will be looking for your first job, returning to the job market after a long absence, or searching for a more challenging position, there is a key to your success—*and that key is a positive attitude.*

1.1   TYPES OF ATTITUDES

Attitudes are usually referred to as:

1. **Positive:** Curious, determined, enthusiastic, honest, optimistic.
2. **Neutral:** Uncaring, apathetic, "I'll just do my time."
3. **Negative:** Defensive, fearful of others' opinions . . . of the unknown . . . of being wrong . . . of taking risks.

1.2   DEVELOPING A POSITIVE ATTITUDE

Believe in your training. Believe in your knowledge, in your skills, and in your ability to communicate with others. *Believe in yourself!* Above all, do not sell yourself short.

Why is a positive attitude important? Many employers believe a negative attitude costs them money in terms of lost production and lower employee morale.

WORLD OF WORK

A supervisor at a manufacturing plant said, "One negative person can infect fifteen other workers." He went on to say that after two negative workers were dismissed, following verbal and written warnings about their negative attitudes, production increased and the remaining employees' attitudes improved greatly.

Because a positive attitude is such a critical factor contributing to job success, a good place to start is by asking yourself some general questions about your attitude. Is it positive? Negative? Neutral? To determine this, complete the following exercise.

TOOLS OF COMMUNICATION

Part A Mark your responses to six statements.

Part B Give this page to someone who knows you well, is in your program, or works with you. Ask that person to mark how he or she perceives your attitude.

Part C Compare your analysis of your attitude with the other person's perception of your attitude. Are there differences or areas where you might develop a more positive way of thinking?

Evaluating Your Attitude, Part A

Instructions: Mark an X on the number you think best describes you. After marking your response to each item, go back and connect the X's with a continuous line. The higher numbers toward the right indicate a more positive attitude. Is your attitude: Positive? Negative? Neutral? (Check one of these three options after connecting the X's.)

	1	2	3	4	
I dislike changes in routine procedures and organized structure.					I enjoy frequent changes in what I do.

	1	2	3	4	
I have difficulty working with people of diverse backgrounds and beliefs.					I like working with people of diverse backgrounds and beliefs.

	1	2	3	4	
It is difficult to listen to people who disagree with me.					I listen carefully when someone expresses an idea or opinion that differs from mine.

	1	2	3	4	
When someone points out my mistakes, I tend to close up or yell at them.					When someone points out my mistakes, I usually am able to listen and evaluate what they say objectively

	1	2	3	4	
When I meet new people, it's hard to know what to say.					When I meet new people, I am comfortable talking to them.

	1	2	3	4	
It's difficult for me to communicate with those in authority (employers, instructors).					I enjoy communicating with those in authority.

Overall, my attitude is:

☐ Negative   ☐ Neutral   ☐ Positive

TOOLS OF COMMUNICATION

Evaluating Your Attitude, Part B

Instructions: Please rate how you perceive my attitude. Be honest, so that I can learn about myself from your assessment. Thank you in advance for your thoughtful evaluations and answers.

Put an X on the number that you think best describes me. After marking your response to each item, go back and connect your X's with a continuous line. Higher numbers reflect a more positive attitude. How do you perceive my attitude. Positive? Negative? Neutral? (Circle one.)

	1	2	3	4	
Dislikes changes in routine procedures and organized structure.					Enjoys frequent changes and working out details along the way.
Is uncomfortable working with people of diverse backgrounds and beliefs.					Prefers working with people of diverse backgrounds and beliefs.
Has difficulty listening to people with differing opinions.					Listens carefully when someone expresses an idea or opinion that differs.
Gets upset and either closes up or yells when someone points out his or her mistakes.					Usually listens and evaluates carefully when mistakes are pointed out.
Is uncomfortable and quiet when meeting new people.					Is comfortable when talking to new people.
Has difficulty communicating with those in authority (instructors, employers).					Communicates easily with those in authority.

In the space below, please write a short response about your analysis of my attitude.

_____

_____

What are my communication strengths in this career field? Please suggest some areas for growth in communication:

_____

_____

Signed by evaluator, _____

TOOLS OF COMMUNICATION

Evaluating Your Attitude, Part C

Instructions: Compare your personal attitude survey with the one you received from the other person. Where do they agree? Disagree? Is there anything you would like to change? What are your communication strengths and areas for growth?

_____

_____

_____

_____

_____

_____

_____

_____

_____

_____

_____

_____

_____

_____

_____

_____

_____

_____

You may have made some poor choices or mistakes, but if you can learn from them, you will benefit from those negative experiences. The only way to grow and learn is to have the attitude, "I want to take risks and learn from my mistakes." Tom Jeske, a carpentry instructor, emphasized this point when he told a student who was repairing a project, "A mistake is only a mistake if you don't fix it." Often you can change a situation by modifying your attitude toward it, even if you cannot alter what has happened.

Remember:

Be INQUISITIVE

NOT INFERIOR OR INDIFFERENT!

Your attitude is the food you choose to serve your mind! If you find your "attitude food" is not very flavorful, you can do something to improve the taste. What can you do? Try some of the ideas in the next section.

1.3 IMPROVING ATTITUDES

If you are in the neutral or negative zone, try the following idea to develop the more positive attitude that is so necessary for success both during an employment interview and later on for success in your career.

Even if you have a generally positive attitude, it will be very helpful to keep an attitude log throughout your life and review it when you encounter a "down" time. Dan Miller, a motivational speaker and polio survivor, encourages us to be "dream makers, not dream breakers." This can happen only when we are willing to persist in our efforts to reach our goals by maintaining a positive attitude.

Can a positive attitude really pay off?

WORLD OF WORK

Gil Leon, vice president of Motor Works, an engine remanufacturing company, hires many employees with no mechanical experience. All that is required, Leon points out, is "Attitude, attendance, and the ability to learn."

Incidentally, this company shared 30 percent of one year's profits with its 80 employees, 12 days before Christmas. The employees' bonus checks, which varied according to length of employment with the company, ranged from $180 for those with three weeks of employment to $8,000 for those with a three-year employment history at Motor Works. The total of the profits the company shared with its employees was $428,000! (Boggs, 1996)

TOOLS OF COMMUNICATION

Attitude Log

Instructions: At least three times a week during the next three weeks, write down something positive that happened to you or to someone around you. This could be something as simple as a good meal or as complex as developing a new design.

Week 1: 1. _____

2. _____

3. _____

Week 2: 1. _____

2. _____

3. _____

Week 3: 1. _____

2. _____

3. _____

TOOLS OF COMMUNICATION

Restoring a Positive Workplace

Instructions: Working in pairs or teams, think of negative comments you have heard or situations you experienced that contributed to a negative work environment. Then decide how these comments or situations should have been managed to contribute to a positive workplace. Share your results with the class.

If you are working alone, interview two employers who hire people in your career area. Ask them how they handle employees who contribute to a negative atmosphere. The results of these interviews can also be shared in class.

To maintain a positive outlook during your job search, try the following ideas:

- One way to improve your attitude is to read. Your mind acts on what you feed it, so read motivational materials or stories about those who have made building blocks out of roadblocks. Then analyze what you have read. Ask yourself, "Why and how did this person succeed? How can I apply this author's ideas to my life?"
- Cultivating friendships with people who maintain a positive view of life will also be helpful. Negative relationships can affect a person very quickly. While you are looking for employment, you do not need to hear discouraging words.

WORLD OF WORK Employers in technical fields such as a fluid power company in Seattle, Washington, and Bonneville Power in Spokane, Washington, emphasize the fact that they do not even want to *interview* prospective employees who have negative attitudes or are untrained in the area of communication.

1.4 JOB SKILLS ASSESSMENT

Once you have analyzed your attitude, it will be useful to assess your personal job skills and determine where and how you developed those skills. This assessment is important because interviewers want to know which skills you will contribute to their company. These skills, often referred to as **transferable skills,** also known as *soft skills,* are specific skills useful in any career. You will need to be able to discuss them confidently with potential employers.

TOOLS OF COMMUNICATION

Transferable (Soft) Skills Assessment

Some employers look for action-oriented words (verbs) such as *analyze, analyzing, analyzed* in resumes, cover letters, and interviews, while others prefer noun forms like *analyzer.* Researching the companies is critical before you send your resume, so you will be certain about their preferred style usage. The following list gives verb and noun forms for the skills you might want to include in your resume.

Instructions: In the first column, circle the skills you possess naturally or have acquired through education or experience. Add more skills as you think of them.

Verb	Action Form	Past Tense	Noun
1. Analyze	Analyzing	Analyzed	Analyzer
2. Begin	Beginning	Began	Beginner
3. Calculate	Calculating	Calculated	Calculator
4. Compare	Comparing	Compared	Comparer
5. Compute	Computing	Computed	Computer
6. Construct	Constructing	Constructed	Constructer
7. Contribute	Contributing	Contributed	Contributor
8. Convey	Conveying	Conveyed	Conveyer
9. Counsel	Counseling	Counseled	Counselor
10. Create	Creating	Created	Creator
11. Demonstrate	Demonstrating	Demonstrated	Demonstrator
12. Design	Designing	Designed	Designer
13. Determine	Determining	Determined	Determiner
14. Develop	Developing	Developed	Developer
15. Diagnose	Diagnosing	Diagnosed	Diagnostician
16. Edit	Editing	Edited	Editor
17. Evaluate	Evaluating	Evaluated	Evaluator
18. Examine	Examining	Examined	Examiner
19. Function	Functioning	Functioned	Functionary
20. Lead	Leading	Led	Leader
21. Listen	Listening	Listened	Listener
22. Manage	Managing	Managed	Manager
23. Observe	Observing	Observed	Observer
24. Operate	Operating	Operated	Operator
25. Organize	Organizing	Organized	Organizer
26. Participate	Participating	Participated	Participant
27. Perform	Performing	Performed	Performer
28. Problem solve	Problem solving	Problem solved	Problem solver
29. Research	Researching	Researched	Researcher
30. Sell	Selling	Sold	Seller
31. Support	Supporting	Supported	Supporter
32. Teach	Teaching	Taught	Teacher
33. Understand	Understanding	Understood	Understanding
34. Write	Writing	Wrote	Writer

6.

Employment Strengths

_____

_____

_____

_____

_____

_____

7.

EXPENSES   Rent/Mortgage

Food

Electricity/Gas

Water

Phone

Job

Inst
skill
inco

_____

_____

_____

_____

_____

_____

_____

1.5   REVIEWING THE PAST

Now it is time to examine your *specific* job experiences. Within every job, there may be activities you like and others that you dislike. Suppose you like writing reports but hate filing, or enjoy calling people to make appointments but dislike answering the phone when others go to lunch. Obviously, then, the skills you will transfer to a new job are writing and spending time talking to people, but you will want to avoid a position that requires filing or answering calls. **"Job Analysis," Part A** gives you the opportunity to review two previous jobs.

Then look at this review of the past from a different perspective. **Part B of the job analysis** asks you to determine the values that would be important to you when you evaluate a new position. **Part C** offers you the opportunity to state your strengths and preferences in two concise paragraphs.

When carefully thought out, the exercises can help you identify some of your specific employment needs and preferences. Please answer these questions carefully. The answers may help you to realize *what you need* in an employment situation, as well as *what you have to offer* to an employer.

TOOLS OF COMMUNICATION

Job Analysis, Part A

Instructions: What kinds of employment have you had in the past? List two jobs you have held, either part-time or full-time. What did you like and dislike about these jobs? (Use words and phrases.)

Job #1—Description	Things You Liked	Things You Disliked
_____	_____	_____
_____	_____	_____
_____	_____	_____
_____	_____	_____
_____	_____	_____

Job #2—Description	Things You Liked	Things You Disliked
_____	_____	_____
_____	_____	_____
_____	_____	_____
_____	_____	_____
_____	_____	_____

Did you supervise anyone else? If so, what did you enjoy about supervision? Or do you prefer a job that does not require you to supervise others?

_____

_____

_____

_____

Job A

1. *At*
   you

   _____

   _____

   _____

   _____

2. *Wc*
   you

   _____

   _____

   _____

   _____

3. *Do*
   wo
   mo

   _____

   _____

   _____

   _____

   _____

   _____

4. *Do*
   Ex

   _____

   _____

   _____

   _____

   _____

5. *Wh*
   are

   _____

   _____

   _____

   _____

Job Analysis, Part D

Instructions: Next, ask yourself which of the following **values** are most important to you in a job. Check the three most critical values. Below the list of values, state why the three you chose are the most significant to you.
For me it is vital that my job has:

- ☐ 1. Good pay
- ☐ 2. Creativity
- ☐ 3. Security—this company is going to be in business long term
- ☐ 4. Medical benefits
- ☐ 5. A good retirement plan
- ☐ 6. Little supervision
- ☐ 7. Structured supervision
- ☐ 8. Support for honesty
- ☐ 9. Support for integrity
- ☐ 10. Recognition for work well done
- ☐ 11. Regular work evaluations from supervisors
- ☐ 12. Support for loyalty to customers and coworkers
- ☐ 13. Other values not listed above

_____

_____

_____

_____

_____

_____

_____

_____

_____

_____

    This **values** assessment can help you understand what is important to you in terms of your needs. If your needs cannot be met by this employer, it will be difficult for you to maintain a productive attitude.
    Now you are ready to investigate your preferred style of **communication.**

1.6 COMMUNICATION STYLES

It's helpful to analyze **communication styles** to see how you compare with others in the class, in the office, or on your work team. When you understand differences in communication styles, you can adjust your communication style to interact with others more effectively. Using communication styles effectively allows you to recognize and accommodate others' styles and motivate people according to their individual strengths and needs.

TOOLS OF COMMUNICATION

Analysis of Communication Styles

Instructions: To begin to understand your preferred style of communication, finish this communication analysis.

The statement that best describes you, rate a	7
The next best description, rate a	5
The third most applicable analysis, rate a	4
The statement that least describes you, rate a	2

1. Others are likely to see me as:

   _____ a. useful and action-oriented.

   _____ b. sentimental and interesting.

   _____ c. reasonable and thoughtful.

   _____ d. rational and a deep thinker.

2. When dealing with others who have an opposing opinion, I can often get to a decision by:

   _____ a. finding one or two ideas to combine with others' ideas to solve problems.

   _____ b. understanding others emotionally.

   _____ c. remaining relaxed while helping others to see things reasonably.

   _____ d. trusting my own skills to put ideas together.

3. I am happy when I:

   _____ a. am able to complete more work than what was planned for the day.

   _____ b. understand the emotions of others and help them.

   _____ c. explain issues systematically.

   _____ d. try new ideas that can be connected to other concepts.

4. When I work on plans, I usually:

   _____ a. want to be certain the plans have results that are realistic to prove that my time and energy will be well spent.

   _____ b. want to be involved in exciting, energetic conversations with others.

   _____ c. focus my energy on seeing that ideas are developed in an organized manner.

   _____ d. want my ideas to bring something original to the project.

5. When thinking about the use of time when communicating with someone, I think most about:

   _____ a. I've got a lot to do; is it worth my time now?

   _____ b. It is worth my time now because relationships are an important part of life.

   _____ c. I'm sure if I take the time to converse now, I will gain information to help me in the future.

   _____ d. It is worth it because I find conversation an interesting, creative, original way to spend my time.

6. It is easy to persuade others when I am:

_____ a. practical and do not talk too much.

_____ b. understand others' feelings as well as my own.

_____ c. reasonable and tolerant.

_____ d. rationally aware of others and able to consider many different opinions.

When you finish this analysis, add the figures in each of the categories (a, b, c, d) and place that number below:

Sum of a's _____   Sum of c's _____

Sum of b's _____   Sum of d's _____

Your highest score will show your preferred style for communicating with others, and your second highest score points out your secondary style. The "a" score implies a *practical* style, the "b" score an *emotional* style, the "c" score an *analytical* style, and the "d" score a *creative* style.

Table 1.1 explains efficient and inefficient uses of each of these styles of communication. These explanations can also assist you in creating a more productive work environment, because you will be able to utilize each coworker's strengths and recognize communication skills that need to be "sharpened."

TABLE 1.1	Characteristics associated with the communication styles.

A. PRACTICAL STYLE	Efficient Application	Inefficient Application
	Useful	Doesn't see long range
	Assertive, directional	Wants attention
	Results-oriented	Self-involved
	Objective	Acts first, then thinks
	Competitive	Lacks trust in others
	Confident	Domineering
	Opinion is based on what is actually seen	

A person with this style of communication could **fear being taken advantage of.**

A person with this communication style probably could be **motivated by directness and confrontation.**

If this is your communication style you will usually be **more effective if you learn to get others' opinions, then move forward.**

B. EMOTIONAL STYLE	**Efficient Application**	**Inefficient Application**
	Spontaneous	Impulsive
	Persuasive	Tries to manipulate others
	Empathetic	Overpersonalizes, takes things too personally
	Understands traditional values	Sentimental
	Probing	Postponing
	Analyzes self	Guilt-ridden
	Draws out feelings of others	Stirs up conflict
	Loyal	Subjective

A person with this style of communication could **fear loss of security due to changes in procedure or policies and/or hurting others.**

A person with this communication style probably could be motivated by the use of traditional procedures.

If this is your communication style you usually will be **more effective if you do not take yourself too seriously and realize you cannot please everyone.**

C. ANALYTICAL STYLE	**Efficient Application**	**Inefficient Application**
	Effective communicator	Talks too much
	Takes time making decisions	Indecisive
	Careful	Overly cautious
	Weighs alternatives	Overly analytical
	Stabilizing	Unemotional
	Objective	Not energetic
	Rational	Controlled and controlling
	Analytical	Too serious, rigid

A person with this style of communication could **fear criticism of work, loss of harmony.**

A person with this communication style probably could be **motivated by the right way to proceed.**

If this is your communication style, you will usually be **more effective if you take risks. Be flexible, willing to move without knowing all the details.**

(continued)

D. CREATIVE STYLE	Efficient Application	Inefficient Application
	Original	Unrealistic
	Imaginative	"Far out"
	Creative	Fantasy-bound
	Broad-gauged, thinks about big picture	Scattered
	Charming	Sneaky
	Thinks about future	Out of touch
	Thinks about theoretical issues	Insistent on own way
	Sticks to theories	Impractical

A person with this style of communication could **fear loss of approval.**

A person with this communication style probably could be **motivated by recognition and praise in front of peers.**

If this is your communication style, you will usually be **more effective if you listen more and organize yourself.**

How do you make use of this information? The situation below illustrates how this analysis can be put into practical use.

WORLD OF WORK

Charlie, a manager, completes the communication styles analysis. His Practical communicator score is within two points of the very different Emotional style of communication. In other words, he recognizes the work that needs to be accomplished and yet is aware of the problems another person may be having at home that are causing him to be absent, thus delaying work. This situation will probably cause Charlie some inner stress, because he clearly understands the demands of the job as well as the needs of the employee. Recognizing the source of the stress can help Charlie make more realistic decisions through getting others' opinions before decision-making time and realizing that a manager can't please everyone.

TOOLS OF COMMUNICATION

Applying Communication Styles

Instructions: Work with a partner, and decide how each person in the following situation could be more effective in the application of his or her communication style. Then compare your solutions with those of the rest of the class.

1. Jane, an Analytical team leader, has to complete a research assignment with her partner, Jack, who is very Practical in his style of communica-

tion. Jack just wants to finish the work and go home. If you were the leader in this situation, how would you motivate Jack?

2. Ken is the leader and probably the most Creative person on the design team. He insists on presenting his ideas to the supervisor even though three members of the group do not think his ideas are Practical. How could these three approach Ken to motivate him to be more Practical? Should they talk to the supervisor about their ideas if Ken ignores them? How could that be accomplished in a positive way?

1.7   WHAT DO EMPLOYERS EXPECT?

About now, you may be asking yourself,
"Why bother with all this self-analysis?"

When interviewing prospective employees, **65.7 percent** of the **329** employers in a year 2000 survey* reported that the **communication skill** most affecting the outcome of the interview was whether applicants could describe their background and qualifications clearly. When asked to indicate the three communication skills most affecting job interviews, employers ranked the skills as shown in the table below. The self-analysis steps in this chapter are essential because they help you learn to communicate your abilities, assets, and attitudes effectively.

* The survey appears at the end of this chapter. A detailed analysis of the survey is available from the author, whose address is listed in the preface.

TABLE 1.2	*Employer ranking of communication skills.*
Number of Employers Responding	**329**
1. Ability to describe their background and qualifications	217
2. Positive nonverbal communication	182
3. Ability to listen attentively	144
4. Ability to state personal goals clearly	114
5. Ability to express ideas enthusiastically	112
6. Other	37
7. No answer	3

In the current job market, however, many significant changes are taking place. These have to do with the changing nature of work.

WORLD OF WORK

Douglas Jardine, retired president of Capilano College in Vancouver, British Columbia, observed:

> Somewhere, not that long ago, I read something to the effect that a competitive world has two possibilities: You can lose. Or, if you want to win, you can change.
>
> A very recent echo of this assertion was made by George Hancock, president of a Canadian firm, when he said, "I don't suppose that there's a company . . . that hasn't changed some fundamental way, whether it's what they produce or how they produce it. Everybody that failed to change ain't here anymore."

(Jardine, 1996)

1. The nature of work is changing. Increasingly, workers need more knowledge skills than manual skills. Products are "robo-factured" rather than manufactured, and workers must be able to plan the work of the robot rather than simply manipulating a tool. The changing nature of work thus demands changes in the nature of education.

2. "Work" is replacing "jobs." The pattern of full-time, full-year jobs is giving way to work on a part-time basis, and often to contract work rather than as an employee. The educational response here must recognize that entrepreneurial skills are a condition of success for the self-employed and are a great advantage to those who work for an employer.

(Leadership Connections, p. 3)

3. It is helpful to evaluate your skills. Evaluate and upgrade your skills and, if possible, consider learning new skills such as speaking another language or inventing a new product or service in order to market yourself more aggressively in the new "workplace without jobs." The term "workplace without jobs" is used by Dr. William Bridges in his challenging book *Jobshift* to describe a widespread phenomenon in the job market: the tendency of employers to hire temporary and/or task-related workers instead of traditional full-time employees.

1.8   APPLYING THE CONCEPTS

All of this self-analysis may produce stress in your life, so stop and try the following idea to reduce your stress level. You may be feeling like a wire that's overstretched and past its limits. If you do, look for "Stress Less" suggestions in each chapter.

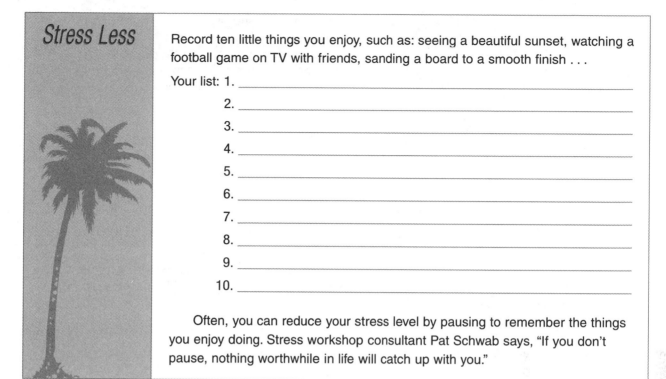

Stress Less

Record ten little things you enjoy, such as: seeing a beautiful sunset, watching a football game on TV with friends, sanding a board to a smooth finish . . .

Your list:
1. _____
2. _____
3. _____
4. _____
5. _____
6. _____
7. _____
8. _____
9. _____
10. _____

Often, you can reduce your stress level by pausing to remember the things you enjoy doing. Stress workshop consultant Pat Schwab says, "If you don't pause, nothing worthwhile in life will catch up with you."

CASE STUDY

A young new employee, Jane, has been exceeding all expectations and seems to be destined for an early promotion. She has a positive attitude toward work and tells others, "I am working for the Johnson Company, not for $10.50 per hour."

Now Jane comes to you and says she is going to quit. When asked why, she says it is because the older employees are so negative that coming to work every day has become increasingly depressing. She wants to find someplace to work where other employees have a more positive attitude. If you were her supervisor, what would you do?

CHAPTER PROJECT

Begin your network of potential employers. Call two employers in your career field, and ask them if they would be willing to complete a communication skills survey as part of a class project. If they agree, copy the survey at the end of this chapter and either mail the surveys or deliver them personally to the employers. Include the name and address of the company for verification of the assignment, and ask the employers to sign the survey. Provide self-addressed, stamped envelopes for the employers to use to return the survey to you. When the surveys come back, tabulate the results and share the outcome with your class. Finally, tabulate the results for the entire class, and discuss the conclusions of this research. Be sure to send the employer a note of thanks.

Performing this survey offers you the opportunity to network with employers in your field to start building your list of possible employers.

Building a broad-based network of employers can be very helpful to you during your job-seeking process. Start constructing your network by keeping a record of your initial contacts and their responses to the surveys. As you meet other employers or hear them speak at an employment fair, add them to your list, thus widening your network of potential employers.

DISCUSSION QUESTIONS

1. Do you think a positive attitude is important in the workplace? Why or why not?
2. Which three transferable skills do you think are the most valuable?
3. Do you agree with the analysis of your communication style? Why or why not?
4. If you were an employer, which three communication skills in question number 1 of the employers' survey would you think are the most important? Why?

SUMMARY

In this chapter you had the opportunity to begin your job search with the following activities:

- You examined your attitude and learned how to improve and maintain it.
- You analyzed your transferable job skills, previous employment, and communication styles.
- You learned what communication skills employers expect during job interviews.
- You looked at recent trends in the changing workplace.
- You began to build an employment network.

COMMUNICATION SKILLS SURVEY

Please help us be of greater service to you.

In an effort to train students more effectively in the areas of verbal communication skills and computer usage, and to better meet your needs as an employer, we would appreciate your assistance. Will you please take a few minutes to answer this brief survey?

1. When interviewing prospective employees, the communication skills that most affect the outcome of the interview are their: (circle three)
   a. Ability to describe their background and qualifications
   b. Ability to state personal goals clearly
   c. Ability to express ideas enthusiastically
   d. Ability to listen attentively
   e. Positive nonverbal communication (such as handshake, eye contact, or general appearance)
   f. Other _____

	ALMOST NEVER	SOMETIMES	OFTEN	FREQUENTLY
2. The applicants I have interviewed have been able to describe their technical skills clearly.	■	■	■	☐
3. The applicants I have interviewed have had a good opinion of themselves as individuals.	■	■	■	☐
4. My decision to hire someone has been affected by the candidate's ability to communicate well during the interview.	■	■	■	☐
5. Most of my employees are able to express their opinions effectively when in a small group (3 to 10 people).	■	■	■	☐
6. It is important that my employees are able to express their opinions in a small group.	■	■	■	☐
7. Most of my employees are able to organize and present a short (5- to 10-minute) speech to a group of 20 to 50 people.	■	■	■	☐
8. It is important for my employees to organize and present a short (5- to 10-minute) speech to a group of people.	■	■	■	☐

9. The communication skills I desire most in my employees are: (circle three)
   a. Following directions efficiently
   b. Getting along with other employees
   c. Communicating with customers effectively
   d. Accepting criticism nondefensively
   e. Communicating in a small group productively
   f. Other _____

10. Please rank the three most important communication skills as they affect the success of an employee in your organization. Rate the most important skill as number 1.

_____ Listening

_____ Prepared speaking

_____ Thinking and speaking on your feet

_____ Employee-to-employer communication

_____ Problem solving

_____ Other _____

11. Please rank the three most important computer skills you desire in your employees. Rate the most important as number 1.

_____ Keyboarding

_____ Online banking

_____ E-mail

_____ E-mail courtesy

_____ Point of sale

_____ Internet access

_____ Word processing

_____ Basic Windows literacy

_____ Database

_____ Accounting software

_____ Spreadsheets

_____ Presentation software

_____ Other _____

_____ Depends on the position(s) such as

_____

_____

For items 12–15, circle the number that most closely pertains to your company.

12. An employee would be dismissed because she or he did not follow verbal directions.

1	2	3	4
almost never	seldom	often	frequently

13. An employee would be dismissed because she or he did not listen to and/or relate well with the customers.

1	2	3	4
almost never	seldom	often	frequently

14. An employee would be dismissed because she or he did not get along well with other employees.

1	2	3	4
almost never	*seldom*	*often*	*frequently*

15. The number of people employed by this business/industry is:

1	2	3	4
1–20	*21–50*	*51–99*	*over 100*

Employer's name _____

Position _____

Name of company _____

Address _____

_____

☐ Please check the box if you want a copy of the survey results.

Community service   Cub Scouts, Cubmaster
_____

Hobbies/interests   Bowling, rock climbing
_____

Honors/awards   Outstanding NCO 1998, McConnell AFB, KS
_____

Career goals (optional)
_____

Personal information   Committed to quality control
_____

References

At least **THREE.** Include name, position, address, phone, e-mail, and fax.

1. Name   Jim Math

    Position   Shop Foreman

    Company   Jim's Fabrication

    Work address   463 S. Holly St.

    City   Peabody   State   KS   ZIP   44777

    Work Phone   913/564-4733   Fax   913/564-7432

    E-mail   jmath@abcd.com

2. Name   Paul Johnson

    Position   Owner

    Company   Johnson Steel Bldg.

    Work address   5834 N. River St.

    City   Harp   State   KS   ZIP   47377

    Work Phone   913/563-0997   Fax   913/563-0709

    E-mail   paulj@hotshot.net

3. Name   Brian Smith

    Position   Welding Instructor

    Company   Hutchinson Community College

    Work address   1500 W. Boyd

    City   Newton   State   KS   ZIP   47454

    Work Phone   913/284-6240   Fax   none

    E-mail   bsmith@abcd.com

The final resume developed from this worksheet appears on pages 47–48.

Now complete the following resume worksheet for yourself.

TOOLS OF COMMUNICATION

Instructions: With this worksheet, begin collecting and organizing information for your resume. **This is not a final form,** but it does list several categories for you to consider. You may not need all of them. Your resume should look *quite different* from the worksheet when you finish it. **Remember,** when writing about your education and work experience, *always list the most current information first.*

RESUME WORKSHEET

NAME (in caps)

Address

Town   State   ZIP

Phone   Fax   E-mail

Education

Institution   Year

Degree   Major

Experience

Job title   Dates

Company

City   State

Fax   E-mail

Skills/duties

_____

Job title   Dates

Company

City   State

Fax   E-mail

Skills/duties

_____

Job title   Dates

Company

City   State

Fax   E-mail

Skills/duties

_____

Equipment operated

A well-constructed, error-free, easy-to-read resume says a great deal about you. It is worth investing time in your future to build one. But the cover letter is also crucial. *Never* send a resume without a company-focused cover letter.

An *original* cover letter discussing how you can serve the unique functions and needs of the prospective employer should accompany each resume. "The basic function of the cover letter is to make the reader curious enough to read the resume," states John Adams, director of career services at Washington State University. In turn, the resume's real function is simply to make employers curious enough to want to meet you. Chapter 3 discusses cover letters in more detail.

2.3 RESUME FORMATS

Once you have completed the resume worksheet, you need to decide which types of resumes you want to use. Not all employers want the same style of resume, so developing two or three will make your job search go more smoothly.

In the past, employers expected to see one of two types of resume. The **chronological** resume lists your education and work experience according to dates, with the most current information always listed first. Note the examples of chronological resumes on pages 38–46. The **skills** (functional) or **assets** type of resume describes your skills and abilities according to categories. This type of resume usually does not list previous employers. The format can be useful if you are changing career fields, have a minimal employment record, or have employment gaps. Some employers prefer this style, but others consider it to be too vague. See examples on pages 47–53.

Another type of resume combines these methods of organization. The **combination** resume contains both functional and chronological information. It focuses on your skills and explains how and where you demonstrated using them. A number of employers believe this format is the best. For examples of this style turn to pages 54–56.

A more recent approach to resume writing is the **online resume,** which appears in a format that is appropriate for the Internet. (See the examples on pages 57–59.) An online resume has a wider and faster distribution to employers and can be more objective than other types. Sometimes the online resume is scanned by an optical character reader (OCR) rather than a real person. To design an online resume, you can start with your regular resume and select key words from it. Some of the key words recognized by employers (Kennedy & Morrow, 1995) who utilize resume-scanning software are:

Ability to delegate	Industrious
Ability to plan	Open communication
Accurate	Organizational skills
Adaptable	Problem solving
Communication skills	Results-oriented
Detail-minded	Safety-conscious
Follows instructions	Team building
High energy	

Ken Smith (1995), coordinator of the Hotel and Restaurant Management program at Colorado State University, compares an online resume to a traditional resume in the following way:

Standard Resume	Electronic Resume
Should be grammatically perfect and free of typographical errors.	Should be free of typographical errors—the computer does not scan for errors.
Centered, with good black print and balanced white space all around.	Use sans serif fonts (like Helvetica); avoid complex layouts.*
Highlight with bolding, underlining, and italics.	No boldface, script underlines, or lines of any kind.
Concise—one page usually is enough.	One page is appropriate for recent graduates. Including more key words can increase your chance of being selected, so longer can be better.
State your professional objective.	Forget the objective, as such; instead, use a key word summary.
Use full spellings for all words.	Abbreviations and industry buzzwords are acceptable.
Pack the resume with "action words."	Use **key words** throughout.

* Dr. Mary Ellen Guffey (1995) suggests using 10- to 14-point Times Roman type because touching letters or unusual fonts are likely to be misread. For the same reason, she advises avoiding double columns.

Before you submit a resume, whether by mail, e-mail, or Internet, check the company's Web page to find out about current requirements, job opportunities, and the preferred resume format. Internet company research can be a vital part of your job search, because it will provide up-to-date information on constantly changing requirements. Do not limit your Internet inquiries to large corporations; many smaller companies have Web pages. In addition, the Internet offers many comprehensive resources for job searches. Some of these are:

www.brassring.com   www.dice.com

www.monster.com   www.hotjobs.com

WORLD OF WORK   According to Kevin Donlin (2001), managing editor of *1 Day Resumes,* for best results on job-search Web sites, you should re-post your resume every 30 days. "Why? When your resume is 'freshly posted,' you appear as a candidate who's actively pursuing a new job, which makes you more attractive to employers."

WORLD OF WORK   Currently, the Boeing Company, with operations in many states, has a pre-designed, fill-in-the-blanks computer resume format for applicants, whether or not a position is available (Internet, January 2001).

4. You may wish to save twice: once on your hard drive and once on a floppy.

5. Change title to "[Your Name] Resume."

6. Change file name to "[Your Name] Resume."

7. Click on **Save.**

TO CONVERT AN HTML FILE TO A WORD (.DOC) OR RTF FORMAT

1. Open the file in a Web browser.

2. Click on **File.**

3. Click on **Edit with Microsoft Word.**

4. In Word, click on **File.**

5. Click on **Save As.**

6. You may wish to save twice: once on your hard drive and once on a floppy.

7. Change type to "Word Document" or "Rich Text Format."

8. Click on **Save.**

TO SAVE A WORD (.DOC) FILE IN AN ASCII FORMAT

1. Open your resume in Microsoft Word.

2. Click on **File.**

3. Click on **Save As.**

4. You may wish to save twice: once on your hard drive and once on a floppy.

5. Change type to "Text Only."

6. Click on **Save.**

7. A message will state that some of the features of your file are not compatible with the text-only format.

8. Click "Yes" to change to the "Text Only" format.

9. Close out this file.

10. Open the text file in Notepad to check and adjust the layout. This file will not look at all like the Microsoft Word document. The words will be the same, but the layout will need some modification.

2.4   CHOOSING YOUR RESUME FORMAT

Study the sample resumes in this section. Each format is unique, and each has different strengths and weaknesses. All of the resumes were originally developed by students; only the names, addresses, telephone numbers, and other identifying details have been changed.

Some employers may use an evaluation form like the one on page 62 to rate the resumes they receive, so study that form to determine what information should be included in your resume.

After finding out what information to include and deciding which styles best fit your background and training, use one or a combination of two or three formats as a basis for your first draft. A well-crafted resume cannot be completed in one, two, or even three sessions. Just as building a house involves a multi-step process because there is much activity that takes place between floor plans and finish work, resume building is also a multi-step process.

When your first printed draft is complete, refer to the resume checklist on page 61 to look for areas that need to be added or revised. You might wish to ask someone else to read your resume and point out errors and omissions. Most people need to go through **at least three** working drafts after finishing the resume worksheet before they send the final version to an employer.

Developing two or three different formats for your resume is a good idea. This will allow you to submit the most appropriate resume for each position. Occasionally you might submit more than one resume for a position in different formats. It will be useful to have chronological, skills, and online resumes in your files, as well as on a computer disk. Be sure that you **always** have a backup disk stored in a separate location in case the first disk is misplaced or goes bad.

WORLD OF WORK   A student's backpack was stolen from her car. The backpack contained her disk, backup disk, and the only printed copy of her work. She had no other option but to start over from the beginning. Lesson learned? Store your backup disk in a separate location, and save yourself a lot of repetitious work.

Chronological Resumes

TED McDERMONT

Box 3756, Spokane, WA 99276

(647) 766-8686 • tmcderm@msn.net

OBJECTIVE   To obtain a position in the computer industry utilizing training and experience.

EDUCATION   Will graduate with an Associate in Applied Science degree in Computer Programming, Spokane Community College, 2002

WORK EXPERIENCE

1998–2000   **INX Industry,** Seattle, WA. Quality control, responsible for checking for quality of computer packaging and parts.

1996–1997   **Redding Computers,** Spokane, WA. Computer sales, purchase orders, maintenance of keyboards.

1995–1996   **Lee Keyboards,** Spokane, WA. Keyboard assembly, minor repairs, Career Path Services.

LEADERSHIP   **Student Awareness League,**
Spokane Community College
Elected President 1998–2000
Treasurer 1997

AWARDS   **Student Awareness League,**
Outstanding Achievement Award for the number one club of the year

REFERENCES   **Matt Gender,** Computer Instructor
Spokane Community College
North 1810 Greene Street
Spokane, WA 99207
(509) 563-6734 Fax: (509) 565-8971

Melissa Newman, Office Technology Instructor
Spokane Community College
North 1810 Greene Street
Spokane, WA 99207
(509) 563-6734 Fax: (509) 563-4587

Angela White, Communication Studies Instructor
Spokane Community College
North 1810 Greene Street
Spokane, WA 99207
(509) 563-6734 Fax: (509) 565-4712

Michael M. Kannegaard

East 4785 Tenth Avenue
Spokane, Washington 99206

(567) 759-4756
michaelk@fastmail.com

Job Objective

Obtain a position in the electronics field with opportunity for advancement to a management position.

Education:

Winter quarter 2000 to present, Spokane Community College, Spokane, Washington
Major: ELECTRONICS
Areas of studies completed: DC and AC theory, active devices and fundamentals of amplifiers, IC concepts both linear and digital, digital systems both hardware and software.

Employment History:

1998–2000   **Guard Security Services,** Spokane, Washington
POSITION: General Manager
DUTIES: Supervised office, sales, and guard personnel. Periodically performed roving and stationary security patrols.

1995–1997   **Tractor and Equipment Company,** Spokane, Washington
POSITION: Field Mechanic/Power Generation Technician
DUTIES: Troubleshooting and repair of generators and diesel engines on oil drilling rigs.

1994–1995   **USCGC Sunnyview WJL 473,** Duluth, Minnesota
POSITION: Chief Engineer
DUTIES: Supervising the engineering department. Administering the operating budget. Implemented the preventative maintenance program.

1991–1993   **USCGC Confidence EMEI 573,** Dokiak, Alaska
POSITION: Assistant Chief Engineer
DUTIES: Responsible for the electrical and structural repair division. Preparing training plans for personnel, including training in electrical/electronics troubleshooting.

Prior Position: Maintenance, repair electrician on various Coast Guard and Navy units, from 1975 to 1995

**Special
Projects:**   Field Sports Director at Boy Scout Camp, Newport, Washington.
Managed Enlisted Men's Club, Coast Guard Base, Seattle, Washington.
Operated the Fleet Post Office, Iwo Jima, Japan.

References:

Shelly Links	Don Smith	Dean C. Kane
East 8578 Happy Road	North 1810 Greene Street	East 1406 Maple Street
Spokane, Washington 99205	Spokane, Washington 99207	Spokane, Washington 99207
(567) 574-4756	(574) 556-5680	(567) 586-7844
Fax: (567) 574-8921	Fax: (567) 556-8217	Fax: (567) 586-6724
Position: Gerontologist	Position: Boy Scout Executive	Position: Electronics Instructor

Frank James

58463 N. SUNNY DRIVE, ROSWELL, NEW MEXICO 88201

(505) 584-8068 • FAX: (505) 584-5274 • FRANKJAMES@EARTHLINK.NET

CAREER GOALS

To improve machinist skills and move into tool and die work

EDUCATION

Associate in Applied Science degree as a machinist 2002, and industrial first aid 2001.

2000—Roswell Community College, Roswell, New Mexico. Machine shop, shop math, blue print reading, knowledge in metallurgy, drilling, lathe operating, milling, grinding, digital readout experience, and knowledge of CNC programming and operating.

1998—Graduated from Roswell High School, New Mexico.

EMPLOYMENT

June 1998–Present **GIBLER TOOL AND DIE**
Production work machining 100 to 1200 parts at a time. Hardinge Automatic Chucker experience, Hardinge Manual Chucker experience, and Bridgeport Mill work.

April 1996–June 1997 **PERFECT GRINDING AND TOOL**
Sharpen end mills, shell mills, roughing cutters, saws, drills, step drills, center drills, 135/1350 split point drills and taps.

June 1995–March 1996 **CAMP CHEVROLET**
Put away stock orders, ship parts, and other miscellaneous duties.

HOBBIES

Fishing, Archery Hunting, and Camping.

REFERENCES

Keith Lane	Jim Johnson	Darrin Wines
Machine Shop, Instructor	Machine Shop, Instructor	Gibler Tool & Die
Roswell Community College	Roswell Community College	790 S. Houk
610 N. Broad Street	610 N. Broad Street	Roswell, NM 88201
Roswell, NM 88201	Roswell, NM 88201	(505) 574-0534
(505) 567-8934	(505) 893-2122	Fax: (505) 574-5214
Fax: (505) 567-3751	Fax: (505) 893-5398	

DAVE C. HIGHLOW

Current Address
5745 E. 8th
Spokane, WA 92746
(573) 456-6778

Permanent Address
2674 N. Houk
Colville, WA 75673
(574) 684-5746

CAREER GOALS: To perform technical and mechanical evaluation of fluid power components, eventually advancing into sales and outside troubleshooting.

EDUCATION: Will graduate from Spokane Community College, June 2002, with Associate in Applied Science degree in fluid power technology.

WORK EXPERIENCE: Associated with large-scale family farming operation. Service and repair of all types of farm-related equipment. Also involved in budgeting and accounting functions.

EQUIPMENT OPERATED: Combines, wheel tractors, and large trucks.

LEADERSHIP: Associated Student Council Representative, Spokane Community College, Spokane, WA, 2001–Present.

Student Body President, Colville High School, Colville, WA, 1998–1999.

AWARDS: Voted Most School Spirit, 1997
Perfect Attendance, 1995–1996

REFERENCES:

John Crocker

Chairman, Fluid Power Department
Spokane Community College
N. 1810 Greene Street
Spokane, WA 99207
(509) 536-7118 Fax: (509) 537-8247

Tom White

Teacher and Rancher
Colville High School
Colville, WA 75673
(574) 785-5745 Fax: (509) 785-4287

Gray Smith

Teacher and Rancher
Colville High School
Colville, WA 75673
(574) 574-7986 Fax: (509) 574-8366

Wilks, Debra J., page 2

EDUCATION   NYU—1998, Art History
Boston University—1996, Economics and Government
Stanford University—1991–1993, Foreign Language

WORK EXPERIENCE

Secretary for John J. Eck, attorney-at-law.
Security guard for multimillion-dollar art collection, Art Gallery, Expo.
Employed by Filene's for storewide inventory.

ESTIMATE OF POTENTIAL

Confident that past experience has developed expertise in dealing with people, promoting sales, organizing fund-raising events, and coordinating large functions. Feel qualified to enter the job market in fields related to office management, public relations, convention/tourist trade, and sales promotion. Would consider additional college education with on-the-job training to give maximum performance. Equipped with maturity and imagination to meet challenges.

INTERESTS   Backpacking, gourmet cooking, crocheting, music, and theater.

REFERENCES

Bob E. Ants, Headmaster
St. Selby's School
43 West Smith Road
Rome, NY 54389
(315) 589-6987 Fax: (315) 567-2398

Ginny Red, National Committee Member
World Service Council
473 East 22nd Avenue
Rome, NY 48488
(315) 347-3840 Fax: (315) 567-8751

Mike L. Lanes Jr., Assistant Vice President
John Lynch, Inc.
4734 West Main
Rome, NY 47377
(315) 574-5967 Fax: (315) 598-4518

George Joggle, Upper School Principal
St. Selby's School
43 West Smith Road
Rome, NY 54389
(315) 589-6987 Fax: (315) 526-6578

JERRY T. PELTES III

305 WEST LIBERTY AVENUE (520) 487-8659
FLAGSTAFF, AZ 86001 JERRYPELTES@YAHOO.COM

EDUCATION

2000–2002   Flagstaff Technical College, Flagstaff, AZ 86001
Associate in Applied Science, Fluid Power Specialist
Graduation: June 15, 2002

SKILLS AND ABILITIES

- Effectively trained to use wide variety of hydraulic and pneumatic equipment
- Various machine and equipment repair abilities
- Proficient in use of Microsoft Office software including Word, Excel, and PowerPoint
- Comprehensive knowledge and experience with AutoCAD R13, R14 software
- Familiar with assortment of fluid power components, including servo and proportional technology
- Extensive electrical training related to field, including circuit design and machine wiring
- Knowledge of digital electronics, PLC's, and microprocessors
- Trained in PLC programming
- Qualified in Industrial First Aid and CPR
- Basic training in Oxy-Acetylene, Arc, and MIG welding

WORK EXPERIENCE

Automotive and Delivery	Manual Labor	Hospitality
Automotive repair	Roofing application	Line cook
Loading/unloading trucks	Mason's assistant	Specialty cook
Truck driver	Rotating stock	Dishwasher
Forklift operator	Power tool maintenance/repair	Stocking shelves
Local delivery	Pulling warehouse orders	
Parking lot attendant	Sprout/tofu production	

REFERENCES

Norman Smith	Will Edwards	Jack Johnson
Fluid Power Instructor	Fluid Power Program Director	Owner
Flagstaff Technical College	Flagstaff Technical College	A-1 Roofing
1018 Browne Street	1018 Browne Street	2942 N. Maxwell
Flagstaff, AZ 86001	Flagstaff, AZ 86001	Flagstaff, AZ 86001
(520) 535-7317	(520) 535-7319	(520) 768-0272
nsmith@xyz.com	willedwards@junomail.com	jjohnson@hotmail.net

BRUCE BOLINGER

21115 S. Pine Rd.

Jackson, MI 49201

(517) 466-9813

serate@devbec.com

Career Goals

To work in a field related to networking for computers, ultimately with the goal of working in network design, routing, and switching in small to enterprise class networks.

Education

- Will graduate from Jackson Community College in June 2002, Associate in Applied Science degree in network engineering. President's/vice president's honor roll every quarter since entering college, earning a 3.5 GPA.
- Graduate of Cisco Networking Academies in Spring 2001, average test score of 93%.
- Additional vocational training in general computer technology earned at Jackson Area Skills Center.

Additional Skills/Certifications

- Cisco Certified Network Associate (CCNA) achieved March 2001. Testing results, 888/1000 indicated strong abilities in routing and security.
- Microsoft Certified Professional (MCP) in Windows 98 achieved in December 2000 with a score of 918/1000.
- Two years Linux experience with Redhat, SuSE, Slackware, and Mandrake distributions in server and workstation configurations.
- Four years experience, NT Server/Workstation versions 3.5x to Server/Workstation 4.0, as well as college training.
- Six years OS/2.x–4.0 experience.
- Nine years, various DOS 3.x–6.x experience.
- Novell 3.x–4.x experience and college training.
- Varying experience, Windows versions in networked environments.
- MCSE and CAN certifications in June 2000.
- Experience and knowledge of 10base2, 10baseT, 100baseT, and Token Ring (4mbit over STP) topologies in routed, switched, and shared configurations.
- Nine years, varying Internet experience and online experience.

Work Experience

2000–present. Employed by Health and Environmental Sciences Division of Jackson Community College. Conducted faculty and student training, computer troubleshooting, hardware configurations, and computer setups using imaging tools such as PQDI, as well as manual software configurations.

Bruce Bolinger, page 2

1999. Employed summer at Jackson Area Skills Center. Minor administration of Novell servers. Set up and administered Windows NT 3.5x and 4.0 (beta) servers and workstations. Maintained computers throughout the building running Windows 95 and Windows 3.11. Set up computer hardware and software, and minor network cabling jobs. Also specified equipment to be purchased for the building computer lab.

Other Interests

Hobbies: Working on cars, reading, creative writing, and wandering around the Internet.

References

Walter John
Computer Technician
Jackson Community College
Liberal Arts Division MS 3100
2015 N. Oak St.
Jackson, MI 49201
(517) 533-6308
wjohn@jcc.jackson.cc.mi.us

Harriet David
Instructor
Jackson Community College
BCS Department MS 3100
2015 N. Oak St.
Jackson, MI 49201
(517) 533-7829
hdavid@jcc.jackson.cc.mi.us

Mack Thomas
Retired
5712 S. Cedar
Jackson, MI 49201
(517) 623-9227
htes@aol.com

Combination Resumes

Keith Jay Ribbles

North 1984 Collins Road
Hyannis, MA 99456
(781) 987-0976
kjay@coldmail.net

SUMMARY OF QUALIFICATIONS

- International representative with strong professional background in labor relations, contract negotiations, arbitration, grievance and dispute resolutions.
- Proven effectiveness in human relations, with ability to establish rapport quickly, interview effectively, and accurately assess people's needs.
- Excellent communication skills, demonstrated competency to deal successfully with people under stressful situations. Well-developed verbal and written communication skills, organize information efficiently, and write in clear, concise, and easily understood terms.
- Professional, well-organized, disciplined, and persistent, with credible public image and also work effectively in high-pressure environment. Stay calm under stress, respond quickly when required, and develop solutions to problems.

EDUCATION

Currently attending Cape Cod Community College, enrolled in business management with emphasis on Personnel Management, 1999–2001

Attended Cape Cod Community College, 1996

Attended Gordon College, Wenham, MA, 1994

EMPLOYMENT EXPERIENCE

1996–1998   **Leasing Manager,** Mico Leasing, Woods Hole, MA
Managed over-the-road trailer operations, with responsibility for all day-to-day business decisions, including filing, bookkeeping, record keeping, sales and maintenance, collections, and correspondence.

1993–1995   **Special Procedures Technician,** Mercy General Hospital, Hyannis, MA
As special procedures technician, duties were to assist in surgery and in emergency room as time permitted.

MILITARY EXPERIENCE

1993–1995   Hospital Corpsman and Independent Duty Specialist, and Survival Medicine Instructor, Hospital Corpsman Fleet, U.S. Marine Force

Keith J. Bibbles

LEADERSHIP

Elected Secretary, Moose Lodge, Council 8704.

Den leader and pack assistant, Cub Scout, Pack 678.

Hobbies include golf, fishing, and camping.

REFERENCES

Ruth Smith
Director, Early Learning Center
Cape Cod CC
Hyannis, MA 99876
(781) 553-7615
ruesmith@abcd.net

Tom Jones, Auditor
3698 North 8th Road
Hyannis, MA 99876
(781) 385-3475
tjones@hotmail.com

Todd Kohl
Assistant Division Director
Mico Leasing
3746 65th Southwest
Newton, MA 99876
(781) 473-6784
toddk@juno.net

CHRIS R. JOHNSON

5208 Downriver Dr. C-206   (818) 848-1590
Glendale, CA 91208   CRJ2222@msn.com

Objective   To work in a radio or TV network environment as a sportscaster to challenge and advance current communication skills

Education   Currently enrolled in classes at Glendale Community College. Will be graduating from California State University Fresno with a Bachelor of Arts degree in communication and a minor in journalism. Associate in Arts degree, Glendale Community College.

Activities   Active member and former president of African American Organization at GCC. Former basketball player at Glendale Community College. Donate time to the West Central Community Center coaching children's basketball team. MESA association in high school.

Experience   September 2000–April 2002   *Sales Rep, Assistant Manager*
Sunburst Electronics, Glendale, CA 91208
Assist manager in placing phone orders, dealing with customers and supervising store during evenings.

June–September 2000   *Office Assistant,*
Glendale Community College   *New Student Orientation Leader*
Various office duties such as: filing, receiving phone calls, and reproducing copies. Conducted new student orientations to assist students in feeling more comfortable in college environment.

April–September 1999   *Parts Specialist*
Sears, Glendale, CA 91208
Shipping and handling various electronic parts throughout California.

References   Mary R. Gibson, *Sales Rep.*   Sally Johnson, *Manager*
Sears   Sunburst Electronics
4700 N. Wall   4602 N. Utah
Glendale, CA 91208   Glendale, CA 91208
(818) 248-6569 Fax: (818) 248-8475 (818) 248-7321 Fax: (818) 257-6342

Denise Smith, *Diversity Specialist*
Institute for Extended Learning
3305 S. Fort Brown Dr.
Glendale, CA 91208
(813) 353-5032 Fax: (818) 257-3877

Electronic (Online and E-mail) Resumes

OWEN C. THOMAS

Summary:
* Relate well to the needs and wants of guests in the hospitality industry.
* Communicate effectively in person and on the telephone.
* Adept in the use of computers.
* Able to acquire business routines rapidly.
* Perform productively under stress.
* Problem solve effectively in emergency situations.

OWEN C. THOMAS
204 E. 4th Avenue
Bellevue, WA 99023
206-923-1627
othomas@ctc.com

OBJECTIVE:
Looking for new horizons, challenges, and opportunities for advancement to management within the hospitality industry, where personal experience can benefit an employer.

EXPERIENCE:
1994–Present
Front Desk Assistant, Head Bellman
The Bellevue Club, Bellevue, WA
A hundred-year-old private club with two dining rooms, eighty-bed hotel, three bars, and athletic facilities.
* Provide room service for club guests.
* Respond to members' requests in person and on the telephone.
* Assist in the bar, espresso machine, kitchen, and/or dining room as needed.
* Responsible for end of shift cash receipts.

1993–1994
Cashier/Work Study
Spokane Community College Culinary Arts Restaurant
* Responsible for guest checks and payments.
* Accountable for all money collected and balanced, with daily computer-generated reports and deposits.

(continued)

1980–Present

Family Business

Clark Custom Caning and Refinishing

* Supervise employees in restoration of antique and modern furniture.
* Provide repair estimates.
* Schedule pickup and delivery services.
* Sell supplies.
* Record bookkeeping accounts on computer.

EDUCATION:

Spokane Community College

Associate in Applied Science degree 1994

Hotel Restaurant Management

President's/Vice President's Honor Roll

CERTIFICATES:

Speech Communication

Applied Food Service Sanitation

Industrial First Aid

REFERENCES:

Duane Aspen

Front Desk Manager

The Bellevue Club

1002 W. Ironwood Drive

Bellevue, WA 99023

(206) 416-1100

Richard Gregg, Instructor

Culinary Arts

Orlando's Restaurant

Spokane Community College

N. 1810 Greene St.

Spokane, WA 99207

(509) 533-1027

Bill Plant

Businessman

21824 E. 24th

Kent, WA 99307

(416) 289-1802

Owen C. Thomas

othomas@ctc.com

HARRY J. DANIEL

528 E. Center Ave.
Canton, OH 44706
(330) 467-2497, hjdaniel@home.com

SUMMARY:

* Productive member in self-directed work team environments
* Highly developed written and verbal communication skills
* Knowledgeable in computer systems and infrastructure technology
* Advanced analytical and problem solving skills
* Accelerated learner, adapting quickly in critical situations

OBJECTIVE:

To provide professional support in computer network technology for corporations, businesses, and their clientele

EDUCATION:

Stark State College of Technology, Associate in Applied Science degree 2001, Computer Network Engineer, *President's Honor Roll*

CERTIFICATIONS:

* CCNA Cisco Certified Network Associate
* MCSE Microsoft Certified Systems Engineer
* MCP Microsoft Certified Professional
* CNA Certified Novell Administrator
* CompTIA A+ certified

EMPLOYMENT: 1994–Present Timken, Canton, Ohio

NOTABLE:

* Designed residential home: From green site, plan revision, to finish construction
* Wrote inside proposal that secured $1 million grant for equipment upgrade
* Managed $300K Alaskan high school casework project; no errors
* Network engineer program, SSCT: 3.98 G.P.A.

REFERENCES:

Al Boschma	Fred Polello	Nancy Herman
Regional Mgr., Starbucks	Supervisor, Timken (retired)	Instructor, Network Engineer
508 E. Stark Ave.	8301 E. Euclid Avenue	Stark State College of Tech.
Canton, OH 44720	Canton, OH 44706	6001 N. South St.
(330) 587-1562	(330) 628-1259	Canton, OH 44720
aboschma@aol.com	fpolello@msn.com	(330) 635-8671
		nherman@hotmail.com

FIGURE 2.3   *Transmission of an e-mail resume.*

Position Vacancy 4 - 203

Send Now Send Later Save as Draft Add Attachments Signature ▼ Options ▼ Rewrap

From: aerocrafter (John Wincek)

To: @ roberts@coldmail.com

Cc:

Subject: Position Vacancy 4 - 203

Attachments: *none*

Charcoal Smaller **B** *I* U T

Dear Mr. Roberts,

Here is the resume we discussed on the phone today. I am also sending you a hard copy by regular mail. Please let me know if you need any additional information.

CENTRALIA MARQUEZ
634 East Norway Ave.
Santa Cruz, Jamaica 99003
Phone: 819-967-5328
cmarquez@scj.edu

OBJECTIVE
Entry-level paralegal position with a prominent law firm

EXPERIENCE
Winter 2002
Office Assistant: Quavle and Quaker
  * Scheduled clients
  * Typed the minutes of meetings
  * Proofread important documents

Sept. 1997-Oct. 2001
Receptionist: City of Santa Cruz
  * Part-time director, Department of Corrections
  * Accuracy of typed documents and other important paperwork dealing with criminal actions
  * Representative for 18-person work unit on the correctional dictation committee
  * Reason for leaving job: To pursue college degree full time

EDUCATION
Feb. 1996-Present
Pursuing a Bachelor of Administrations
  * Expected graduation date: May 2002
  * Attended full-time from 1995 until 2002 while working part-time
  * Financed 100% of all college expenses through a scholarship

PERSONAL DATA
  * Assisted in starting the Race and Cultural Equality for Work Association at Santa Cruz University and served as president fo two years; secured the writer of _I Know Why the Caged Bird Sings_ as speaker
  * Traveled throughout Asia
  * Member of the Administration Society
  * Willing to relocate

NOTE
A fully formatted hard-copy resume version is in the mail.

GRAMMAR AND MECHANICS NOTES

- Notice that nouns are featured in this e-mailed resume.
- "Only ASCII characters are used; all text is one size with no special formatting; no rules, graphics, columns, tables, and the like are used . . . Lists are formatted with asterisks instead of bullets" (Ober, 2001, p. 536).

2.5 RESUME CHECKLIST

DO INCLUDE:

✔ Name, address, phone, fax, e-mail
✔ Appropriate wording for degrees/certificates
✔ Educational specializations
✔ Experience—most current first
✔ Action words to describe work
✔ Correct abbreviations such as WA, MA
✔ Bullets to draw attention to important details
✔ Goals (optional)
✔ References, using complete address, position, phone/fax/e-mail

DON'T INCLUDE:

✔ The word "resume"
✔ Just a job title
✔ Marital status, height, weight
✔ Hobbies, unless you are lacking information
✔ Salary figures
✔ Meaningless abbreviations (etc. and so on)
✔ So much information that the pages appear crowded

Even if you e-mail your resume, you can also print it on a good quality of paper, and mail it to the employer or bring the copy to the job interview.

WORLD OF WORK

During an interview, a technical job recruiter commented on the excellent paper quality of a resume when an applicant presented it in person after it was previously faxed.

WORLD OF WORK

Is the style of printing on a resume important?
During a pre-employment interview, the personnel manager for a robotics company said he will not even *read* a resume if it is printed on plain paper or has poor quality print.

2.6 GRADING RESUMES

As was mentioned earlier, some employers use a grading sheet to evaluate resumes, often in order to determine which candidates to invite for interviews. Other employers grade the resume after the interview. Most employers have some way of ranking resumes, and they often circle key words or even errors on the resume itself.

You can better understand this grading process if you try it yourself.

TOOLS OF COMMUNICATION

Grading a Resume

Instructions: Use this resume evaluation form to determine how you would grade two resumes from this chapter. Compare your grade with your instructor's grade or that of someone else who has knowledge of resume construction. Was your grade similar to the other person's? This evaluation tool is also useful in predicting how employers might evaluate your resume.

RESUME EVALUATION FORM

	POINTS	POOR	FAIR	GOOD	EXCELLENT
1. What was the overall appearance of the resume? (40 points)	☐	■	■	■	☐
2. Did the resume use an appropriate format? (15 points)	☐	■	■	■	☐
3. Were there any mechanical errors (spelling, punctuation, grammar, etc.)? (30 points)	☐	■	■	■	☐
4. Were there any typographical errors? (10 points)	☐	■	■	■	☐
5. Did the resume show the strengths of the potential employee (education, work skills, personal information)? (25 points)	☐	■	■	■	☐
6. Does the resume include references (name, position, address, phone, fax, e-mail)? (30 points)	☐	■	■	■	☐

General comments:

_____

_____

_____

Your points: _____   Total possible points: _____150_____

WORLD OF WORK

An employer for an electrical maintenance company contacted an instructor at the local college to complain about the poor quality and number of mistakes a recent graduate of the electrical program had made on his resume. He went on to say he wouldn't hire anyone who did such sloppy paperwork, no matter how good his or her skills were!

Feedback from others is very useful. Using copies of the resume evaluation form, ask two people to grade your resume before you submit it for a final grade, send it to prospective employers, or take it to job interviews. This process can provide useful feedback about the effectiveness of your resume. Others often will discover errors you may have missed because you are so familiar with your own information. Also, it will be useful to have your resume evaluated by at least one person outside of your class but in your career area. When you receive feedback from someone who has knowledge of your training but does not know you personally, that person's rating will probably be more objective.

For another evaluator, select a person completely unfamiliar with your career field to determine if your employment history and training are presented clearly. This feedback is useful when your resume will be evaluated by someone such as a personnel director. You will want to know if this information can be understood by a person who is not familiar with your training.

What else can be done to differentiate yourself from other applicants? You might want to consider assembling information for a portfolio.

WORLD OF WORK

Following a recent series of interviews for a carpentry position, the journeyman carpenter conducting the interviews asked the interviewees why only one out of the four interviewees had taken the time to organize pictures of his work in a portfolio. He stressed that photographs of work in progress and completed work are excellent methods for showing an employer what you have accomplished.

2.7 BUILDING A PORTFOLIO

"Portfolio" is a word often associated with spies like James Bond, diplomats in foreign countries, or artists, not those in technical or business fields. However, anyone can make a very effective use of a portfolio.

A **portfolio** is a documented, often pictorial record of work that provides a visual demonstration of your specific skills and abilities. This collection of personal accomplishments is something to take with you to show a prospective employer.

How could a portfolio be organized, and what should be included? An attractive $8\frac{1}{2}$ x 11 three-ring notebook (no hearts, flowers, or company logos), with acetate pages in a variety of pocket sizes, works well.

A portfolio is an ongoing project and could include:

■ Photographs of your work, such as a building you helped to construct, a car that was restored, clothing or hair styles you created

- Samples of projects completed, computer designs you originated, or programs you created
- A record of presentations in which you participated
- Awards, certificates, or letters of commendation you have earned
- Copies of projects, flyers, or brochures you designed
- Original writing you produced or documents you developed
- Letters of recommendation
- Self-assessment tools you have used, such as a learning style analysis or a Myers–Briggs personality profile, to give a potential employer a multidimensional picture of who you are

Once you have collected this unique profile of what you can do and who you are, organize it in the notebook.

1. All pictures and samples of your work could go in one section.
2. A record of your awards might occupy another area.
3. Letters of recommendation should be included toward the end.
4. Organize copies of certificates with the most relevant first.
5. Number the pages.
6. Make a table of contents that lists the topics and the starting pages.
7. Include tabs along the side of each topic area for quick access.

WORLD OF WORK

Last year, during a practice interview, a student in a cosmetology department brought a portfolio of her work to show an employer. The employer was very impressed with the photos of the student's fingernail art. In fact, the employer called back to ask the student to come in for a "real" interview. As this situation demonstrates, taking the time to develop a personal portfolio could be very profitable.

2.8 CREATING A WEB PAGE AND A CD

A recent development in the job-seeking market is that candidates have begun to develop personal Web pages to assist employers in evaluating them. The advantage of an individualized Web page is that it is accessible to a wide range of potential employers. By mentioning your Web page in your cover letters, you can provide easy access to information about you.

With a color scanner, you can format the page to include photographs, designs, certificates, or any of the other items mentioned in the section on portfolios. If you do not know how to develop a Web page but believe it would be beneficial, seek out an instructor to teach you how, or find someone whom you can hire to produce your page. Contact a computer department at your local college or university for this information.

Another recent development in the job search process is to create a CD of your Web page or portfolio and give it to the interviewer as a unique record of your education and organizational ability. The CD cover information can be printed with a replica of the Web page cover graphics.

It is important to keep updating your portfolio, your resume, and your Web page even after you secure a position, because you never know when an internal promotion or an opportunity for advancement with another company may occur. With a current resume, an updated portfolio, and an accessible Web page, you will always be ready to take advantage of new opportunities in rapidly changing employment fields.

Stress Less

When you have revised your resume for the third time and the instructor says you still need to make more corrections, try the following stress-reducing exercise.

The One-Minute Vacation

Picture someplace in the world you would like to be—the woods, the seashore, or a mountaintop. Set a timer, and mentally stay in that picture for one minute. If you can relax for even *one minute,* your stress level will go down.

A variation of this "stress less" exercise is to buy a poster or picture of a favorite scene and spend one minute looking at it.

2.9 APPLYING THE CONCEPTS

CASE STUDY

Study two resumes in this chapter from different career fields. Thinking of yourself as a personnel interviewer, list the strengths and weaknesses of these resumes. How would you improve them?

CHAPTER PROJECT

In teams of four or five, study three resumes in this chapter. Each of you should evaluate them separately, using the resume evaluation form. Then, as a team, decide which two people you would call back for an interview. Explain to the rest of the class why you would want to interview these people.

DISCUSSION QUESTIONS

1. What information do you believe is the most important to include in a resume?
2. Which resume formats do you think are the most useful? Why?
3. What would you recommend adding to the resume information to make it more meaningful?
4. What would you add to a portfolio and/or Web page to make it even more relevant for your career field? How about a personal CD?

SUMMARY

In this chapter you learned about:

- Methods and guidelines for organizing information for resumes
- Electronic resumes
- Various resume formats
- Checking and evaluating resumes
- Portfolios, Web pages, and CDs

Armed with this information about yourself, you are ready to research available positions and to prospect for information about companies of interest to you.

3 Creating Interest in Yourself

LEARNING OBJECTIVES

1. Understand the importance of knowing about businesses. Learn how to research them and how to expand your network of potential employers.

2. Practice using various resources for investigating companies.

3. Understand the usefulness of cover letters and the different types of letters.

4. Learn how to evaluate cover letters and practice evaluating them.

5. Practice writing solicited and unsolicited cover letters.

6. Understand the importance of finishing application forms appropriately. Learn the guidelines for filling them out correctly, and practice completing them accurately.

7. Understand what affirmative action forms may contain.

8. Practice applying the concepts.

You may be interested in working for a specific company in your local area, in another state, or even in a different country. But if this business has not advertised a position for someone with your skills, what can you do to get the employer's attention? Researching the company at a library, on the Internet, or with a CD-ROM can give you valuable information. This information will help you write a cover letter in which you can discuss their *type of work* accurately and explain how your training could benefit the company.

Remember to keep records of all employers that you research or contact in the list of potential employers that you started in Chapter 1.

3.1   RESEARCH BEFORE YOU WRITE TO EMPLOYERS

Let's explore some sources of information for researching a company. Incidentally, an additional benefit for you in doing this research is that it will help you to decide if the company is a place where you would want to work.

Getting started with this exploration can be the most challenging part of the job search process. One of the richest sources of information is usually a college or local library. If you will just *ask* for help, most librarians will be eager to assist you.

Two useful books for beginning research are the *Standard Industrial Classification Manual* (SIC Code Manual) and the *North American Industry Classification System*. Available in most libraries and online, these publications are numerical classifications of all types of technical fields and business establishments. The SIC codes were developed by the U.S. government to facilitate collection, tabulation, presentation, and analysis of statistical data concerning employers, the type of workers they employ, what they do, and their economic status. Once you determine the SIC code(s) for your career, you will be able to utilize resources such as these:

Company Directories

1. *Dun's Regional Business Directory*
2. Geographical regional publications, such as:
   - *Northwest High Tech*
   - *Advanced Technology in the Pacific Northwest*
   - *Inland Northwest Manufacturers Directory*
   - *Washington Manufacturers Register*
   - *Oregon Directory of Manufacturers*
3. *Hoover's Guide to Computer Companies* and *Hoover's Guide to Private Companies*
4. *American Big Business Directory*

Internet-Based Resources

1. *Reference USA:* an online directory of U.S. businesses, e-mail library@infoUSA.com.
2. *Hoover's Online:* more than 10,000 company profiles in the corporate directory, searchable by company name, ticker symbol, key word, or even a person's last name. (www.hoovers.com)
3. *HotJobs.com:* submit your resume or scan for jobs on this notable job board. Includes career tips and job profiles. (www.hotjobs.com)
4. *thingamajob.com:* job hunting website allows users to search for open positions and post their resume online. Also provides interview and resume tips. (www.thingamajob.com)
5. *HeadHunter.net:* post resumes and search for jobs for free. Regularly updated database lists more than 200,000 jobs. (www.headhunter.net)
6. *CareerBuilder:* search the jobs database by title, location, or salary. Submit a profile and be notified when jobs matching the description are posted. (www.careerbuilder.com)

7. *ComputerJobs.com - Texas Computer Jobs:* locate thousands of jobs for Web developers, Unix administrators, Windows developers and managers. (www.texas.computerjobs.com)

8. *Internet.com - jobs.internet.com:* Internet and e-commerce portal has extensive listings of job openings in many areas of the Web. Search postings or use the personal search agent. (http://jobs.internet.com/)

9. *Thomas Register of American Manufacturers:* the Internet's largest industrial buying and specifying guide, this site offers access to a large database of industrial information. (www.thomasregister.com)

10. Yellow page directories:

    - Qwest (www.qwest.com)

    - Switchboard (www.switchboard.com)

    - BigBook (www.bigbook.com)

11. With the *American Business* CD-ROM disk and the SIC codes relevant to your career field, you can access almost all of the data listed in various printed sources. This disk allows you to research specific companies in various geographic areas, including information concerning the financial status of that company along with the names, addresses, and phone numbers of the appropriate contact persons.

Other Information Sources

Where can you find additional information about companies and positions? You can:

1. Look in both local and out-of-town newspapers. Read the business section of the papers, as well as the classified ads, to identify trends.

2. Ask your friends for names, and add these names to those you collected in the Chapter 1 employer's survey project to continue to build a network of information.

3. Write or call the chamber of commerce in a town or city where you want to work. Ask for names of employers in that area who hire people in your career field.

4. Use the direct approach by going to companies and businesses:

    - Go to personnel offices, sometimes referred to as human resource offices.

    - Request a tour of the shop or office.

    - Talk to current employees on their break if possible.

    - Make an appointment with the lead supervisor or office manager, ask questions, and make notes of the answers.

5. Go to career, placement, or cooperative education offices on campus.

6. Check state, city, and county offices for advertised openings.

7. Research CD-ROM indexes.

8. Investigate online computer search engines and Web browsers such as Yahoo! (www.yahoo.com), dogpile.com.

9. In addition to the Web sites listed above, the following sites may prove useful in your job search.

Web Site	Addresses
America's Job Bank	www.ajb.dni.us
Brass Ring.com	www.brassring.com
Career.com	www.career.com
Chicago Tribune Career Finder	www.chicago.tribune.com
Contract Employment Weekly	www.ceweekly.wa.com
E-Span Employment Database	www.joboptions.com/jo_main/index.jsp
Federal Government Agencies	www.lib.lsu.edu/gov/fedgov.html
FedWorld	www.fedworld.gov
High Technology Careers	www.hightechcareers.com
International Careers	www.jobweb.com/catapult
Internet Sleuth: Employment	www.yardim.bilkent/edu.tr/Search/Sleuth/empl.html
Job Searching on the Internet	www.wpi.edu/Admin/CDC/Resources/Srchnet.html
MedSearch America	www.medsearch.com
Monster.com	www.monster.com
Web Jobs USA	www.webjobsusa.com
Workplace	www.career.galaxy.com
Yahoo! Finance	www.quote.yahoo.com

10. The Commercial Sites Index (www.directory.net) provides a searchable collection of company and organizational pages, with links to more than 20,000 Web pages.

How can you put this information to practical use? Study the following sample job research project and think of ways you could adapt it to your field.

Sample Job Research Project

Perhaps you want to move to the Pacific Northwest and are trained as a welder. The SIC numbers for that field are: 1799, 7692, 7694, 3715, 3713, 7519, and 7539. The *Thomas Register* of company profiles and the *Thomas Register of Products and Services,* with listings by state and SIC code, list companies that employ welders.

Dun and Bradstreet's Regional Business Directory for the Washington area (Vol. 1) also lists companies by city and SIC code. One of those employers is Reliance Trailer Co.

The following is an example of information you would find in the *Dun and Bradstreet's Regional Business Directory* about the Reliance Trailer Co. (207):

Reliance Trailer Co.
S. 3025 Geiger Blvd., Spokane, WA 99204
Tel (509) 455-8650   Ownership 1998
Sales   16MM   Emp 100
SIC 3715, 3713, 7539 Truck Trailers
Brian Ling, Manager
Steve Miller, CFO
Duke Yole, Mgr

A research information sheet could contain the following data concerning Reliance:

RESEARCH INFORMATION SHEET

1. Name of Company: Reliance Trailer Co.

2. Address: S. 3025 Geiger Blvd. Spokane, WA 99204

3. Phone number: (509) 455-8650, Fax: (509) 747-4811

4. Contact person: Duke Yole, Mgr*

5. Type of work: Truck trailers

6. Additional Company Information: New ownership since 1998, 100 employees

7. Additional Information listed in the *Reference USA* program included:

    Frank Gibler — Plant Manager

    Ron Amatsuo — Sales Executive

    Roy Jeffreys — Purchasing Agent

    Credit Rating — Very Good

Now you are ready to organize information about companies that will be of benefit to you.

TOOLS OF COMMUNICATION

Library Research Project

Instructions: Use this page for your research project. Make as many copies as you need.

SIC numbers for my career area are:

Use some of the resources listed above to complete this form for each company that interests you.

1. Name of local company: _____
2. E-mail: _____
3. Address: _____
4. Phone number: _____ Fax: _____
5. Contact person: _____
6. Type of work: _____
7. Additional company information: _____
   _____

1. Name of company not located in your area: _____
2. E-mail: _____
3. Address: _____
4. Phone number: _____ Fax: _____
5. Contact person: _____
6. Type of work: _____
7. Additional company information: _____
   _____

As a result of your research for each company, ask yourself:

- How do my training, education, and personal skills meet the needs of this company?
- What is the focus of this business? Sales? Research? Manufacturing? Marketing?
- Does the salary scale meet my needs?
- What is the size of the company? Would I be comfortable here?
- Who is in charge of the area where I want to work?
- What is the projected future of this company or business?

Once you have completed the company research portion of the pre-interview process, you are ready to create your cover letter. Remember, the more you know about a potential employer, the greater advantage you will have in focusing the letter on the needs of the company. Knowing specific information about the company will also be beneficial later, during the interview.

WORLD OF WORK

Denise Osei (1995), multicultural specialist, says: "Along with your resume it's very important to include a cover letter about your personal and technical skills, because usually an employer is looking for people with skills they don't presently have, and your resume sometimes lacks the specific information the employer needs to know about you."

3.2 GENERAL FORMAT FOR COVER LETTERS

Each time you write a cover letter, review this format for composing letters to be sure the information you include is complete and accurate.

1. **Use appropriate paper.**
   - Letters should be printed on $8\frac{1}{2}$ x 11-inch white paper or paper of the same color and quality as your resume. *Never* use a dot matrix printer or perforated paper.
   - The envelope should be of paper of the same color as your resume and of standard business size, $4\frac{1}{3}$ x $9\frac{1}{2}$ inches. You may want to use a larger envelope ($8\frac{1}{2}$ x 12 or 11 x 13) for mailing your resume package if you have additional information to include, such as letters of recommendation.

2. **Use appropriate format.** The block-left style simplifies formatting the letter because all of the sections align on the left margin of the paper and you do not have to tabulate across the page, as in some older styles of business correspondence.

3. **Use an attractive arrangement of print on the page.**
   - A 70-space line is probably the simplest.
   - If you do not have a specific person's name to whom you will address your letter, use the AMS style of business letter (see Figure 3.7). In that style, your return address may begin about line 12 from the top of the page. If the job opening was advertised on the Internet, use a similar style but insert the e-mail address in place of the inside address (see Figure 3.8).

4. **Use care in proofreading.**
   - Be sure there are no misspelled words or typographical errors in the final copy and that corrections have been made neatly. When in doubt, use the dictionary or a computer spellchecker to verify spelling.
   - Have others proofread your material. The spellchecker on a computer will not catch all spelling problems, such as the distinction between *their* and *there*.

Your cover letter is an advance salesperson for you. You want it to work for you, so be careful when writing. You want the potential employer to have the best possible impression of you.

FIGURE 3.2   *An unsolicited cover letter to the Reliance Trailer Co.*

504 West Hammer Ave
Newton, KS 67114
October 29, 2001

Mr. Duke Yole
Manager
Reliance Trailer Co.
3025 S. Geiger Blvd.
Spokane, WA 99204

Dear Mr. Yole:

Are you interested in hiring an experienced, dependable worker with practical work experience, as well as someone having recent education in both welding and sheet metal? If so, I may be the person you are looking for. As you can see by my enclosed resume, I also have work experience in several other technical areas.

According to the information about your company listed in the Reference USA program, you have 100 employees. The years I spent in the Air Force taught me how to be both a team player and a team leader with diverse groups of people. With this background, I believe I could adapt quickly to your work environment and be of benefit to the Reliance Trailer Co.

Since I will be visiting family in the Spokane area during the Christmas holidays, I will call to see about the possibility of touring the plant and obtaining an interview with you or someone else. A portfolio with photographs of my work will be available at that time. If you would like any additional information, please call me at (316) 743-5607 between 8:00 A.M. and 3:00 P.M. Central Standard time.

Sincerely,

David J. Jessup

David J. Jessup

Enclosures

FIGURE 3.3 *Unsolicited cover letter.*

980 Robland Avenue
Trail, British Columbia
CANADA V1R 3N1
May 20, 2002

Mr. John Clay
Trifle Equipment Limited
4532 #6 Road
Richmond, BC
CANADA V9X 8T3

Dear Mr. Clay:

I come from an outstanding fluid power technology program. I have received the best training possible the past two years at Spokane Community College, so I believe that I can be an asset to your company.

The fluid power technology program includes extensive work with hydraulic systems interfaced with electrical and pneumatic control circuits, machine shop procedures and welding. In addition to the technical training in fluid power, I have taken courses in job communication skills, leadership development, and industrial first aid.

After researching your company on the Internet and reviewing your Web page, I can see that my training in hydraulics would be a fit for your company. Also, my work and in-class experience have given me the ability to work well with my hands, to develop manual dexterity, to work under pressure at a high level of efficiency, and to work with many types of people.

When you have had an opportunity to read my resume and the enclosed course outline, I will look forward to talking with you regarding an appointment for an interview. Please consider me for a position with your company. I will be in Vancouver during summer break, June 18–28, and could be available for an interview during those days. Also, another date could be arranged if that time is not convenient. If I have not heard from you, I will call you during the second week of July. The telephone number here at Spokane Community College is (509) 533-1111, or after 3:30 p.m., I can be reached at (509) 345-7985.

Sincerely,

Julie Smith

Julie Smith

Enclosures

FIGURE 3.4   *Unsolicited cover letter.*

1924 West 10th Avenue
Boise, ID 83681
February 5, 2001

Mr. Jake Roberts, President
KMS Construction, Inc.
3830 East Boone Avenue
Boise, ID 83670

Dear Mr. Roberts:

I am currently enrolled in the network engineering program at Boise Community College, where I have received training in configuring, installing, and maintaining computer networks. Given the recent growth of networking applications in your industry, I believe that I can be an asset to your company.

The network engineering program has included both theoretical and hands-on training and experience with multiple client-server based networks and diverse operating systems such as Windows 95, 98, and 2000 as well as Novell 5.0 and NT Server. I have taken courses in interpersonal communication, technical writing, and I am currently taking training in job communication skills.

As you can see by my enclosed resume, I have worked in the construction industry intermittently over the last twenty years. As a result, I have a solid background in the building trades. I have also worked in production at Boeing, where I learned to work with people from diverse cultures, languages, and backgrounds and to be part of an efficient, productive team.

After you have an opportunity to read my resume, I can be reached at (208) 838-8964 before 9:00 A.M. and after 4:00 P.M. Mountain Standard time. I will have a vacation break the last week of February and I will call you before that time about an appointment for an interview. I look forward to talking with you soon.

Sincerely,

Max Collin

Max Collin

Enclosure

TOOLS OF COMMUNICATION

Writing an Unsolicited Cover Letter

Instructions: Write a letter to one of the two companies you researched. The letter should not be handwritten and should be error-free. This will usually require two or three revisions. If possible, prepare your letter on a computer so that you can revise it easily. In addition, always keep a hard (printed) copy of your work, so you will have something to refer to if both your backup and regular disks are damaged or lost.

Exchange letters with another person in class and rate each other's letters using the evaluation form below. Your instructor also will probably grade your letter using the same or a similar evaluation form.

Once you have an error-free letter, mail it. Start prospecting while you are still in school. Don't stop with one company—write to two or three. But make certain *each* letter is focused on specific information pertaining to that company.

If you have developed your own Web page on the Internet, be sure to include the e-mail address in your cover letter, along with some specific references to your individual skills and abilities.

UNSOLICITED LETTER EVALUATION FORM	POSSIBLE POINTS	JESSUP'S	SMITH'S	MINE
1. Opening sales appeal	15			
2. Typing accuracy	10			
3. Qualifications, training, personal examples of experience	15			
4. Specific references to the work the company does	20			
5. Grammar, spelling, sentence structure, punctuation	15			
6. Where/when to reach; interview asked for	15			
7. Closing	10			
TOTAL POINTS	100			

3.4 SOLICITED COVER LETTERS

When writing a cover letter for an advertised position, you have an opportunity to present your case effectively. A good solicited letter will show interest, enthusiasm, and knowledge of the company and the position for which you are applying. You also will be demonstrating your ability to use English correctly.

Your solicited letter should contain:

- A clearly stated **request for the position** listed in the advertisement. Include the date and place of the advertisement.
- Your **reasons for wanting to work for the firm,** incorporating what you know about the business.

- A brief statement about **why you think you are qualified** for this position. If you do not match *every* requirement, explain how you could adjust to meet that need or acquire added training.

- A sentence stating that **your resume is enclosed.**

- Information about **where and when you can be reached** for an interview.

WORLD OF WORK

Recently, while completing this project, a student discovered a company with an opening that matched his career interests. Although the job description exceeded his level of training, he e-mailed them his resume with a cover letter describing his skills, which matched what he had learned about the company from its Web pages. As a result of this communication, he received an offer for summer employment by e-mail that same day!

TOOLS OF COMMUNICATION

Evaluating Solicited Cover Letters

Instructions: Either with a partner or individually, read the following two letters and rate them according to the evaluation form on page 85. Which letter is more effective? Do they include enough information? Would you call either one or both for an interview? Explain why or why not.

FIGURE 3.5   *Solicited cover letter.*

1234 East 10th Avenue
Spokane, WA 99306
May 18, 2001

Ms. Joan White
Information Center Manager
Brown Products, Inc.
3329 West Main Street
Seattle, WA 98764

Dear Ms. White:

I am writing to you in response to your ad in the *Seattle Republic* for an entry-level pro-grammer. Perhaps you recall that I telephoned you on Monday, June 1, to inquire about the position. At that time, you invited me to send a copy of my resume, which you will find enclosed in this package along with a sample of some of my recent work.

I have an Associate in Applied Science degree in computer programming. My resume indi-cates the extent of my skills and experience in this area. I believe that I am most qualified as an entry-level programmer and could efficiently fill the position your company is seek-ing to staff. When I found the details of your company listed in the regional directory, *Advanced Technology in the Pacific Northwest,* I realized you were the type of organiza-tion I am eager to become a part of.

As I mentioned in our phone conversation, I am moving to the Seattle area toward the end of June. I would appreciate hearing from you regarding the possibility of an interview. I can be reached from 8:30 a.m. to 2:30 p.m. at the college on weekdays at (509) 533-1243. My home phone is (509) 123-4567.

If I have not heard from you by June 23, I will call to arrange for a possible interview when I reach Seattle. I am looking forward to meeting with you.

Sincerely,

Jeff Brown

Jeff Brown

Enclosure

FIGURE 3.8　*AMS style letter responding to a job opening listed on the Internet with no contact person.*

230 2nd Street S.W.
New Philadelphia, OH 44663
August 22, 2000

VCM Computers
Personnel Department
email//vcmproappo4.jobs/search.htm

REQUEST FOR AN INTERVIEW

On Tuesday, I was browsing the job search site for your company, and I noticed an opening for a Mfg Associate 1. I believe that I could be a person of interest for the job.

For the past two years, I have been attending Stark Technical College in Canton, OH, and have earned a degree through their network engineering program. Through this program, I was able to learn how to read schematics of computers and how to successfully put together a motherboard. I also had the opportunity to take a basic PC class, which has taught me more about the CPU. I believe this training exceeds the requirements in your job description. I am a hard worker and I am ready to make an impact at your company. I am faxing you my resume for any information that you may need.

Please call me at (330) 339-6215 between 9:00 a.m. and 1:00 p.m. Eastern Standard time to set up an interview. I can also be reached by e-mail at groberts@compro.com. Thank you for your time and I look forward to hearing from you.

Sincerely,

Grace Roberts

Grace Roberts

TOOLS OF COMMUNICATION

Writing a Solicited Cover Letter

Instructions: Look in the classified ads in your local newspaper and find a position you would be qualified to fill. Research the company if the name is mentioned in the ad. Write a letter to answer the ad using the suggestions and the format given in this chapter. The letter should be typed and error-free. Two, three, or even more revisions are often necessary in order to develop a high-quality letter.

Exchange letters with another person in class, and rate each other's letters using the evaluation form below. Your instructor probably will also grade your letter using the same or a similar evaluation form.

Before you mail a cover letter, rate your letter on the following factors to see if it gives a correct impression of your skills. It will be very helpful to ask someone familiar with this style of letter to rate it also, so you can get objective feedback about the content of your letter.

RATING YOUR SOLICITED LETTER

	POSSIBLE POINTS	BROWN'S	ALLEN'S	MINE
1. Does the letter refer to a specific ad and date?	10			
2. Sales appeal of the letter	15			
3. Knowledge of the company	15			
4. Typing accuracy	10			
5. Qualifications (training and/or experience) included	15			
6. Correct grammar, spelling, sentence structure	15			
7. Does the letter ask for an interview? Does it include when and where the applicant can be reached?	15			
8. Closing	5			
TOTAL POINTS	100			

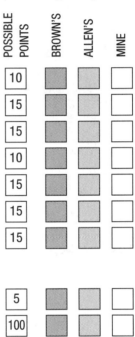

3.5 COMPLETE APPLICATION FORMS CORRECTLY

Learning how to complete an application form is an absolute necessity. If you photocopy some sample forms and practice filling them out, you will be able to take your completed, correct sample form with you to interviews. This practice saves time and ensures accuracy by allowing you to transfer information quickly from the sample form to the prospective employer's form.

Another option is to go to the personnel office ahead of time, ask for the form, photocopy it, and practice filling it out. Once you have a corrected copy of the application form, you can transfer the information to the original. *Be sure to read and follow the directions on the form.* Some employers view the inability to follow simple directions on a form as an indication of a prospective employee's inability to follow directions on the job. They may even dispose of an application form that is incomplete or messy or has misspelled words.

The supervisor for a machine shop said he doesn't mind if job applicants have someone else fill out the application form for them. He just doesn't want to have the form returned with the coffee stains and greasy smudges he sometimes sees. He went on to say that a messy form often indicates a disregard for quality workmanship, and his shop produces high-quality work.

Guidelines for Filling Out Application Forms

When completing application forms always take your personal information with you, such as address, phone number, e-mail address, and social security number. It is also useful to have extra paper and/or a calculator for math problems, a sharpened pencil, eraser, pen with black ink (or an erasable one), and a pocket dictionary. By following the suggestions below you can ensure that your application form is completed accurately and effectively.

1. *Follow directions!* Show employers you can follow instructions.
   - **Read** whether you are supposed to *type, print,* or *write.* If in doubt . . . print.
   - **Read** if you are to use pen or pencil. When in doubt, use a pen with black ink, not pencil or a pen with blue ink. Blue ink and pencil do not photocopy well when duplicates are needed.
   - **Think** before you print. Carefully read all the questions on the application, think of your complete answer, and then print your answer.
   - **Keep** the application neat and clean. Do not scribble, try to black out, or cross out mistakes. If you make a mistake, simply draw one straight line through the mistake and write the correct word next to it or above the error. Well-done application forms should be error-free.
   - **Put** something in every appropriate block or line. If the question does not apply to you, write N/A (not applicable), a short dash (–), the word *None,* or the words *Does not apply.* This shows the interviewer that you are a careful reader and have answered every question on the application form.
   - **Spell** correctly. If you are not sure how to spell a word, try to use another word with the same meaning. That's why you need to take a pocket-sized dictionary with you!
   - **"Place of birth"** means the city and state where you were born, not the name of the hospital.
   - **"Job for which you are applying"** means a *specific* job title or type of work. *Do not* write "Anything." Employers expect you to state clearly what kind of work you can do.

2. **References:**
   - Ask three or four people who will say something good about your work or reliability to be your references. It is more effective to use people not already included in your resume. **Ask** these people if you may use their names *before* you list them. Then ask these two questions: *May I use your name as a reference? Will you give me a* good *reference?*
   - **Do not use parents, relatives, or young friends, but use teachers, older friends, and former employers.**

■ Know your reference's complete name, address, phone, place of business, position in the company, and years known. Include the fax number and e-mail address if these are available.

3. **Keep a record** of all information that **may** be necessary to fill out applications. Take a copy of this detailed information with you whenever applying for a position. This includes:

    ■ Starting/ending dates and addresses for your complete work history, including supervisor's name and reason for leaving.

    ■ Physical limitations if relevant to this employment.

    ■ Machines you can operate.

    ■ Military service (DD Form 214).

    ■ Green card or other evidence of eligibility to work in the USA.

    ■ Computer skills and software.

    ■ Names and addresses of colleges, universities, and schools you attended. Include certificates or degrees awarded along with years and length of enrollment.

4. **Sign your full name.** When asked for your signature, *always write.* **Do not print.** Be sure to use your actual name—baptismal, given, or the name on your Social Security card. **No nicknames** like "Skippy" or "Moose." A signature consists of the following:

    ■ First name
    ■ Middle initial *Donald D. Smithers*
    ■ Family name

Questionable Questions

Do you *have* to answer all the questions on an application form? The answer is a firm *no*. However, some questions that may appear illegal must be answered because they are pertinent to the job.

Illegal	Legal Questions and/or Conditions
What is your age?	Your employment involves serving alcoholic beverages
What is your birth country?	Do you have documentation for working in the USA?
What is your marital status? How many children do you have? Are you pregnant?	Do you have any limitations concerning travel, moving, or overtime? Do you have any expected absences?
What do you weigh? How tall are you?	Since this job requires lifting over 50 lbs and carrying it 100 yards, do you have any physical limitations that would prohibit your doing so?
Was your discharge from the military service honorable?	What type of training did you receive in the Air Force (Army, Navy, etc.)?
Any questions pertaining to ancestry	Do you have any records listed under another name?
Questions concerning race, color of skin, eyes, or hair	None are legal.
Have you ever been arrested?	Have you been convicted of a felony within the last seven years?
What interest groups are you a member of? What church do you attend?	Which business/professional/technical organizations do you belong to?

Remember that the written application form is often the employer's first picture of you and a reflection of the kind of worker you are. Are you neat and detail-oriented or sloppy and careless? Show pride in yourself by filling out the application carefully. This attention to detail might at least get you an interview.

If you are not hired or even called for an interview, many employers will keep your application on file for a period of time, along with your resume and cover letter for future reference. That is one more reason to be sure to complete your application form with the same high quality of workmanship as your resume and cover letter.

TOOLS OF COMMUNICATION

Completing Application Forms Accurately

Instructions: Complete the information on the application form in Figure 3.9. Then exchange your application form and this rating sheet with someone else in class. You may also need to exchange resumes in order to check the application for accuracy.

RATING YOUR APPLICATION FORM	POSSIBLE POINTS	JUDGED POINTS
1. Neat and legible	25	
2. Error-free	25	
3. Accurate	25	
4. Followed directions	25	
TOTAL POINTS	100	

FIGURE 3.9 *Sample application form.*

APPLICATION FOR EMPLOYMENT
(please print plainly)

This company provides equal opportunity in all areas of employment and does not discriminate against any individual on the basis of race, color, religion, sex, age, national origin, marital status, or handicap.

Date _____

Name _____ Soc. Sec. No. _____

Present address _____

City _____ State _____ ZIP _____

Home phone no. (____) _____ Work phone no. (____) _____

Date of birth _____ Are you legally able to work in this country? ○ yes ○ no

Position or type of employment desired: _____

_____

Salary desired: _____

Available for: ○ full time ○ part time ○ temporary Date available: _____

Hours available: _____ Days available: _____

Names of relatives employed by this company: _____

_____

Indicate how you learned of this opening: _____

○ own accord ○ agency (name of agency): _____

Employee referral (name of employee): _____

Other _____

Do you have any physical reasons that would prevent you from performing the specific kind of work for which you are applying?

○ yes ○ no If yes, describe and explain the work limitations: _____

_____

Have you ever been convicted of a felony? (conviction of a crime is not an automatic bar to employment. All circumstances will be considered.)

○ yes ○ no If yes, explain: _____

Military (U.S.) ○ yes ○ no If yes, was the discharge honorable? ○ yes ○ no

If no, please explain the details: _____

(Veterans may be asked to provide a copy of discharge form dd214.)

(continued)

Affirmative Action Forms

Affirmative action forms like the one shown below may be included with some application forms. It will be your choice to complete it or not.

RE: AFFIRMATIVE ACTION

_____ has affirmative action programs for Disabled Veterans and Veterans of the Vietnam Era Veterans Readjustment Assistance Act of 1974 and the Rehabilitation Act of 1973, respectively. If you believe yourself covered by either act and wish to benefit under ("under the provisions of") the affirmative action program, please check the appropriate box below. Submission of this information is voluntary, and refusal to provide it will not subject you to discharge or disciplinary treatment. Information obtained concerning individuals shall be kept confidential, except that (1) supervisors and managers may be informed regarding restrictions on the work or duties of handicapped individuals and disabled veterans and regarding necessary accommodation; (2) first aid and safety personnel may be informed, when and to the extent appropriate, if the condition might require emergency treatment; and (3) government officials investigating compliance with the act shall be informed.

If you are handicapped or a disabled veteran, we would like to include you under the affirmative action program. It would assist us if you tell us about (1) any special methods, skills, and procedures that qualify your handicap or disability, so that accommodations that we could make would enable you to perform the job properly and safely, including special equipment, changes in the physical layout of the job, elimination of certain duties relating to the job, and other accommodations.

○   I am a disabled veteran or veteran of the Vietnam era.

○   I consider myself mentally or physically handicapped.

○   I do not wish to participate in either program.

Comments: _____

_____

_____

_____

_____

_____

VOLUNTARY AFFIRMATIVE ACTION QUESTIONNAIRE

Name: _____

_____, as an equal opportunity employer, has made a commitment to an affirmative action program and is required by state and federal guidelines, including corrective employment programs, to maintain the information. The success of our program depends on your voluntary compliance.

REMINDER: This information will be used only for the purpose of the development of statistics.

ETHNIC:

    O Asian or Pacific Islander   A person having origins in any of the original peoples of the Far East, Southeast Asia, the Indian Subcontinent, or the Pacific Islands. The area includes, for example, China, Japan, Korea, the Philippine Islands, and Samoa.

    O Black   A person having origins in any of the Black racial groups
       (not of Hispanic origin) of Africa.

    O American Indian   A person having origins in Alaska or any of the original peoples of North America, and who maintains cultural identification through tribal affiliation or community recognition.

    O Hispanic   A person of Mexican, Puerto Rican, Cuban, Central or South America, or other Spanish culture or origin, regardless of race.

    O White   A person having origins in any of the original peoples of
       (not of Hispanic origin) Europe, North Africa, or the Middle East.

VETERAN STATUS:

    O Veteran

    O Vietnam era veteran   August 5, 1964–May 7, 1975)

    O Disabled Vietnam veteran Any person whose discharge from the service was for a disability incurred during the line of duty or who is entitled to a disability compensation under the laws administered by the Veterans Administration for a disability rated at 30% or more.

    O Disabled veteran

Dates of service: _____

HANDICAPPED:

    O Yes   O No   Any person who (a) has a physical or mental impairment that substantially limits one or more major life activities, (b) has a record of such impairment, or (c) is regarded as having such an impairment.

    O Male   O Female

Date of Birth (mm/dd/yy) _____

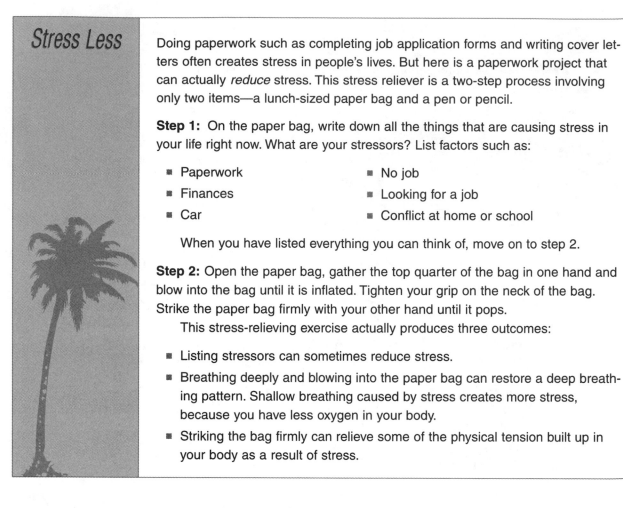

Stress Less

Doing paperwork such as completing job application forms and writing cover letters often creates stress in people's lives. But here is a paperwork project that can actually *reduce* stress. This stress reliever is a two-step process involving only two items—a lunch-sized paper bag and a pen or pencil.

Step 1: On the paper bag, write down all the things that are causing stress in your life right now. What are your stressors? List factors such as:

- Paperwork
- Finances
- Car
- No job
- Looking for a job
- Conflict at home or school

When you have listed everything you can think of, move on to step 2.

Step 2: Open the paper bag, gather the top quarter of the bag in one hand and blow into the bag until it is inflated. Tighten your grip on the neck of the bag. Strike the paper bag firmly with your other hand until it pops.

This stress-relieving exercise actually produces three outcomes:

- Listing stressors can sometimes reduce stress.
- Breathing deeply and blowing into the paper bag can restore a deep breathing pattern. Shallow breathing caused by stress creates more stress, because you have less oxygen in your body.
- Striking the bag firmly can relieve some of the physical tension built up in your body as a result of stress.

3.6 APPLYING THE CONCEPTS

CASE STUDY

With a partner decide how you would resolve the following situation:

Sarah and John have both applied for the same advertised position. According to the resumes, their training and experience are very similar. Sarah also submitted a cover letter that reflected knowledge of the company, but John's cover letter did not mention anything about the company. However, John had an application form that was neat and consistent with the information on his resume, whereas Sarah's form listed employment experience that was inconsistent with data on her resume.

If you were an employer, would you call Sarah or John for an interview? Neither? Both? Explain the basis for your decision.

CHAPTER PROJECT

Working in teams, select a company in your career field, research the company, and, as a team, construct an unsolicited letter that focuses on the company's products or services. When the letter is complete, each team will submit it to the instructor, who will grade each team's effort. Then the class will vote on what they perceive to be the most effective letter in terms of company knowledge, sales appeal, discussion of qualifications, and basic sentence structure, spelling, and punctuation.

DISCUSSION QUESTIONS

1. What are three reasons why it is important to investigate a business or company when applying for a position?
2. What are the disadvantages in using cover letters that are copied from someone else or mass-produced?
3. List four elements that should be included in an unsolicited cover letter.
4. How can you save time when filling out application forms?

SUMMARY

This chapter provided you with experience in the following:

- Researching companies for job opportunities
- Evaluating cover letters
- Writing cover letters for both unadvertised and advertised positions
- Completing application forms correctly and evaluating them

Each of these activities gives you the opportunity to create interest in yourself so that you will be called for a job interview.

4 What Was That You Said? Telephoning and Listening

LEARNING OBJECTIVES

1. Understand and apply effective communication tools when using the telephone to ask about employment.

2. Learn to overcome poor listening habits by practicing effective listening.

3. Learn the importance of feedback tools for listening to others.

4. Practice using direct questions and additional skills to verify information when communicating with others.

5. Understand barriers to successful communication, including some cultural differences.

6. Understand the communication circuit.

7. Apply the concepts.

This chapter explains how you can use the telephone to locate employment possibilities and gives you opportunities to develop productive listening and feedback skills. In one communication skills survey, 274 out of 329 employers stressed the need for employees to have listening skills to deal effectively with customers, coworkers, and supervisors. In fact, those employers selected listening as one of the top three communication skills they desired in their employees (Clark, 2000).

The chapter also presents a brief discussion of communication barriers and cultural differences to make you aware of why some communication problems occur. It closes with an overview of the "communication circuit" to emphasize the role of listening in the communication process.

4.1 USING THE TELEPHONE DURING EMPLOYMENT SEARCHES

When making a telephone call to inquire about a job opening or to request an interview, avoid calling during the first hour of business on a Monday or on Friday or Saturday afternoon. On Monday, most businesses are trying to get work organized, and on the last day of the work week, extra time is often needed to complete projects. Your phone call could be an unwelcome interruption unless the position you are calling about has just been advertised. In that situation, the employer may want a quick response.

Every time you use the telephone, you are actually projecting your presence into somebody's home or office. Your voice should create a favorable impression. Observe the following telephone courtesies:

■ *Before placing a call, have your thoughts well organized.* Then you will be able to proceed in a direct, orderly manner. Write down all your ideas in advance so you will not forget something important. Have necessary reference materials right by the phone, such as information about the position and the company. Your resume and work history should also be available.

■ *Let the phone ring seven to ten times before you hang up.* The person you are calling may be busy and unable to answer your call in three or four rings.

■ *Concentrate on establishing vocal contact to compensate for the lack of visual contact.* Try to sound friendly, yet businesslike.

■ *Call only when necessary, and be brief when you do call.* In business, time means money. Do not call about employment so often that you would be considered an annoyance.

■ *When leaving a message on someone's voice mail or answering machine, speak slowly, distinctly, and directly into the phone.* This is especially important when leaving telephone numbers or any other message involving numbers. Give the date and time of your call. Identify yourself by stating your full name (not just your first name; the person replaying your call later may know several people with the same first name). It is always a good idea to repeat your name and telephone number again just before hanging up.

■ Use the phonetics and number-articulation techniques below to ensure you are understood.

PHONETIC SPELLING

When you are spelling your name, try using the verification list below. The list can also be helpful as you listen to others and want to be sure you have the correct spelling of names or words. This code helps in differentiating between often-confused letters such as B and D, F and S, or B and V. You can verify letters by using the method commercial and military pilots often practice. These phonetics are recommended by the International Telecommunication Union, an agency of the United Nations.

A	Alpha	H	Hotel	O	Oscar	V	Victor
B	Beta	I	India	P	Papa	W	Whiskey
C	Charlie	J	Juliet	Q	Quebec	X	X-ray
D	Delta	K	Kilo	R	Romeo	Y	Yankee
E	Echo	L	Lima	S	Sierra	Z	Zulu
F	Foxtrot	M	Mike	T	Tango		
G	Golf	N	November	U	Uniform		*(continued)*

PHONETIC SPELLING Continued.	For example, the name Brad Fischer could be clarified this way: My name is Brad Fischer—"B" as in "Beta," "R" as in "Romeo," "A," "D" as in "Delta" [pause] "F" as in "Foxtrot," "I," "S" as in "Sierra," "C" as in "Charlie," "H," "E," "R" as in Romeo.

ARTICULATING NUMBERS	When repeating **numbers** to a caller, the proper articulation for the phone number 415-334-2514 is: "Area code four one five (pause) three, three, four (pause) two five (pause) one four." The phone number 702-769-2500 is: "Area code seven zero two (pause) seven six nine (pause) two five zero zero."

When making an appointment for an interview for an advertised position:

1. Identify yourself.
2. Ask if this is a convenient time to call. If not, ask, "When may I call back?"
3. Ask if the position is still open. If so, state your information briefly.
4. If you need to mail your resume, ask for the name of the person who should receive it.
5. If there is no opening, ask whether or not they accept resumes to keep on file. If they do, mail yours to them.
6. Thank the person you spoke with, regardless of the response.

See Figure 4.1 for a graphic summary of possible phone scenarios.

FIGURE 4.1   *Calling regarding an advertised position.*

Hello, my name is Tom Maxwell and I am calling about your advertisement for an electronics technician. Is this a convenient time for me to call?

Yes

No

Is the position still open?

Yes

No

Are you making appointments for job interviews, or do you want me to mail my resume and cover letter?

Mail resume   Making appointments

It does not happen very often, but if you get a yes to the first part of the question, that's great! After scheduling the interview, ask:

May I please pick up an application form ahead of time?

If this is not allowed, take the sample form from Chapter 3 with you for reference.

Who will receive this information? What is his or her position?

If you are unable to get a specific name, ask for the name of the department where your information should be directed.

If I send you my resume, will you keep it on file? For how long?

This is a good question for two reasons:

1. Many companies call people whose resumes are kept in their files before advertising a new position.

2. Perhaps the person they just hired will not work out, and you might be considered for the job if your resume and cover letter are available.

If this company does not keep resumes on file, ask if the company will be hiring soon or if they know of another company needing someone with your skills.

When would be a better time for me to call?

If you are told to call back later, don't assume you know what the person means by "later." Does it mean later today? Tomorrow? In a week? To clarify, ask:

Do you mean later today?

If the answer is yes, verify the time.

What time? *or* Before or after 3:00 p.m.?

If you are calling from a different time zone, confirm which time zone the person is using:

Do you mean East Coast time or Mountain Standard time?

Finally, verify your understanding:

All right, I'll look forward to talking to you today between 3 and 4 p.m.

Always close with a sincere expression of appreciation for the person's time:

Thank you for your time, Mr./Mrs. _____

Always use the person's name during your conversation, because it makes the call more personal and less sterile.

TOOLS OF COMMUNICATION

Telephoning

Instructions: Use an audiotape recorder/player and work in a three-person team. Use this outline to make an appointment for an employment interview. The first person takes the role of the caller.

This person should:

1. Identify himself or herself.

2. Ask if it is a good time to call; if not, determine when it would be convenient.

3. Ask if the position is open.

4. If the position is available, ask who makes appointments for interviews or if you should first send a cover letter and resume.

5. If the position has been filled, ask whether they keep resumes on file.

6. Thank the person.

The second person represents the company and uses one of these responses:

1. Yes, there is a job opening.

2. This is not a convenient time for a telephone call.

3. The position has been filled.

The third team member serves as the observer, who operates the recorder and provides feedback on the rating scale on the following page.

Rotate positions until each team member has a chance to practice asking questions, answering them, and observing. Then each person should listen to the tape and evaluate his or her own telephone techniques. Finally, as a group, discuss effective and ineffective answers, tone of voice, rate of speech, enthusiasm, and so on.

If you are doing this **alone:**

- Practice out loud. (Imagine the employer's responses, or play both roles yourself.)

- Use an audiotape recorder/player to determine how you sound.

- Play it back and listen to yourself, and evaluate yourself on the rating scale. Ask another person to listen to the tape and evaluate you using the rating scale and to give you suggestions.

ANSWERING INTERVIEW QUESTIONS

Interviewee _____

Your name _____

WORDING THE ANSWER	POOR	FAIR	GOOD	EXCELLENT
Used complete sentences	■	■	■	☐
Positive answer	■	■	■	☐
Was specific	■	■	■	☐

VOICE				
Volume	■	■	■	☐
Interest and enthusiasm	■	■	■	☐
Sounded positive	■	■	■	☐
Energy level	■	■	■	☐
TOTAL	☐	☐	☐	☐

Comments _____

_____

ANSWERING INTERVIEW QUESTIONS

Interviewee _____

Your name _____

WORDING THE ANSWER	POOR	FAIR	GOOD	EXCELLENT
Used complete sentences	■	■	■	☐
Positive answer	■	■	■	☐
Was specific	■	■	■	☐

VOICE				
Volume	■	■	■	☐
Interest and enthusiasm	■	■	■	☐
Sounded positive	■	■	■	☐
Energy level	■	■	■	☐
TOTAL	☐	☐	☐	☐

Comments _____

_____

4.2   IS POOR LISTENING A PROBLEM?

How many times have you heard yourself say, "I'm sorry, what did you just say?" or "Would you please repeat that?"

What is the problem? Why do we have difficulty concentrating on what others tell us even when it could mean money in our pockets—like getting a job or a raise? One aspect of the problem is that people often think of communication as *talking* or *writing*. Yet, according to one of the pioneers in the study and research of listening, Dr. Ralph Nichols:

> 45% of our awake time is spent listening
>
> 30% of it is spent speaking
>
> 16% of it is spent reading
>
> 9% of our awake time is spent writing.
>
> (Jones, 1998)

Nichols found that without training we listen with a shocking **25% efficiency!** He also reported that out of any 10-minute briefing, the untrained listener will lose 75 percent of what was said after two hours.

One of the primary causes of listening inefficiency is our "thought speed." Most people can think at a speed of 500 to 800 words per minute, but many speakers talk about 125 words per minute. Consequently, a listener is mentally going someplace about four times faster than a speaker, teacher, supervisor, or customer (Nichols, 1957).

Research conducted by Lyman K. Steil, special listening consultant for the Sperry Corporation, emphasized the cost of poor listening:

> With more than 100 million workers in America, a simple ten dollar listening mistake by each of them would cost a billion dollars. Letters have to be retyped; appointments rescheduled; shipments reshipped. And when people in large corporations fail to listen to one another, the results are even costlier. Ideas get distorted by as much as 80% as they travel through the chain of command. Employees feel more and more distant, and ultimately alienated, from top management.

He went on to report the following alarming statistics concerning the flow of information in business:

When the message originates with the **chairman of the board:**

67% of the message gets to the **vice-president.**

56% of that message from vice-president goes to the **general supervisor.**

40% of the same information from general supervisor is passed on to the **plant manager.**

30% of the message from plant manager moves on to the **foreman.**

BUT ONLY

20% of that original message is received by the workers on the line!

(Sperry Univac, 1983)

As a result of these findings, some large corporations are spending a lot of money to open communication from the bottom to the top by teaching their employees at all levels how to listen more productively.

WORLD OF WORK

This statement in the fluid-power publication *Compressed Air Magazine* (1998) underscores the idea that listening should move in the opposite direction—from the bottom to the top.

Ideally, communication goes upwards, not downwards. It does not begin with managers telling their employees what's what. It begins with the subordinate's interest, then works its way up to the manager, so that the manager will then have something to communicate that is intelligible and palatable to the subordinate. Peter Drucker believes that "Nothing connected with understanding, let alone with motivation, can be communicated downward."

The worst listening habits, according to Dr. Nichols (1957), are:

1. Calling a subject uninteresting or boring
2. Getting excited and judging the message before the speaker finishes speaking
3. Listening for the facts only and not the reasons for those facts
4. Faking attention
5. Tolerating outside noises or interferences that hinder listening accuracy
6. Avoiding listening to difficult material
7. Letting emotion-causing words used by the speaker (such as "you jerk") develop mental interference, reducing our ability to listen rationally
8. Wasting the time differential between speaking and listening. Remember, 125–150 words per minute is the rate of conversational speech, while 500–800 words per minute is your thinking speed.

4.3   OVERCOMING POOR LISTENING HABITS

You can become a better listener by:

Focusing your five senses on the speaker's message. Realize listening is work! Sit up, feel alive, look the speaker in the eye. Listen with concentrated attention to overcome outside distractions. Do not fake attention.

Making sure you have the correct understanding of what the speaker wants to convey. Listen to detect central ideas, not just facts. Ask questions, reword, and verify information. Learn to control your reactions as you listen. Simple awareness of your listening habits will take you a long way toward becoming a better listener. Once you have the correct understanding, you can decide on your opinion and respond accordingly.

Once you make the decision to *really* listen, specific techniques can help you increase your listening efficiency. Following are some methods for improving your listening skills.

THE 10 BEST LISTENING HABITS*

1. Tune in to see what will be of interest to you, even if you think you have heard it all before.

2. Get the meaning of the message, which is much more important than the speaker's appearance, mannerisms, or poor grammar—do not let these things distract you.

3. Hear everything the speaker has to say before you judge him or her.

4. Listen for a brief time before taking notes to determine the critical elements of the message.

5. Listen for main ideas, principles, and concepts, as well as facts.

6. Listen with energy. Relaxing while listening is *not* helpful. In good listening, there is a collection of energy and tension inside of you. When you are receiving directions or during a job interview is no time to sit and nod your head vaguely while your mind is elsewhere.

7. Get up and do something about distractions—shut a window, close a door, ask the speaker to speak louder, or ask the person next to you to be quiet so you can concentrate on what the speaker is saying.

8. Learn to listen to difficult material or different points of view on television and radio to practice the skill of listening objectively.

9. Identify your own greatest verbal and nonverbal barriers. Is it a person's frown or someone calling you "stupid" that causes you to stop listening?

10. Make thought speed an asset instead of a liability by mentally summarizing and analyzing what has already been said rather than daydreaming about your plans for the weekend or planning what you will say next.

* Adapted from Ralph Nichols, "10 Keys to Good Listening," quoted in Jones (1998), pp. 16, 17.

TOOLS OF COMMUNICATION

Practicing Effective Listening Techniques

Instructions: Circle three of the preceding 10 good listening habits you need to develop, and list them below. Use the listening log to check and improve your listening skills during the next week. Bring your log to class. In small groups, record which habits you most need to develop. Do a class tally to determine the most common listening weaknesses. Since all good habits are established through repetition, repeat the exercise for another week.

1. _____

_____

2. _____

_____

3. _____

_____

WORLD OF WORK

"During a job interview, listening well is even more important than answering questions well," points out Sharna Fey, a regional recruiter for the Marriott Corporation.

LISTENING LOG

1. Write down one on-the-job or school situation in the past in which a misunderstanding occurred.

   _____
   _____
   _____
   _____

   ■ What was the listening problem in that situation?

   _____
   _____
   _____

   ■ What could you have said or done to avoid this problem? Record your preferred wording or action.

   _____
   _____
   _____

2. During the next week, list three situations in which you needed to listen carefully. How did you respond? Which good listening techniques did you use? Which ones did you forget?

   _____
   _____
   _____

   Listening situation #1

   _____
   _____
   _____

   Your response:

   _____
   _____
   _____

Listening situation #2

_____

_____

_____

Your response:

_____

_____

_____

Listening situation #3

_____

_____

_____

Your response:

_____

_____

_____

3. Now analyze your listening habits. Do you have trouble following instructions? Why or why not? Do you overreact? Do distractions interrupt your listening?

_____

_____

_____

4. Which *listening* behaviors can you adopt to improve your communication with customers and coworkers? Refer again to the 10 Best Listening Habits. Select at least two more to practice for one more week while you listen to those around you.

_____

_____

_____

Continue trying these ideas over the next few weeks. If you do this consistently, you will undoubtedly see noticeable changes in how others react to you. It has been said that a habit must be repeated **21 times** to become an integrated skill, so keep working to incorporate efficient listening skills as a tool in your communication toolbox.

Characteristics of efficient listeners include:

1. Open-mindedness about people who look or sound different from yourself
2. The ability to follow several methods of organization—even poorly organized material can be listened to with some degree of tolerance
3. The ability to hear conclusions, inferences, and generalizations, along with the facts
4. Listening even more attentively when the material becomes difficult because you see it as a challenge
5. The ability to reword information to clarify your understanding of what someone has said

One conclusion we can draw from these statements is that effective listening is not an easy skill to acquire. It demands energetic involvement and interaction with others. Research has shown that heart rate, pulse, and blood pressure increase when you are truly involved in the listening process (as seen in the film *Power of Listening,* 1984).

 ## VERIFYING INFORMATION: A COMMUNICATION TOOL

Communication feedback tools can help you acquire effective listening habits. One critical feedback tool to use when telephoning, interviewing for a job, or later when relating to others on the job is the skill called **paraphrasing,** or *rewording information.*

We cannot always be sure that our message will have the same meaning to others as it has for us. Most people tend to assume that what they understand from a statement is what the speaker intended. Paraphrasing or rewording the information, is one way to be sure you understand the speaker's message. When you do this, *you are not giving advice or making judgments.* It is a way of saying to another person, "This is what **your** words mean to me."

The two purposes for rewording information are:

- Let the other person know **what you understand** his or her words to mean by checking the meaning.
- Let others know you are interested in what they are saying.

Here is an example of this skill used to check the facts:

Interviewer: I'll meet you at the door after lunch.

You: (to verify) Do you mean inside of the door to the building at 1:00?

Interviewer: No! I meant outside of the door to the shop at 12:30. We take a lunch break at 11:30.

You can see the importance of clarifying meaning. Otherwise you could end up in the wrong place at the wrong time. Don't assume you know what the other person means. Verify!

Why Do You Need to Reword Information?

This technique increases the accuracy of communication. It provides feedback by confirming what the other person's statements mean to you. Obviously, we cannot restate everything others say, but there are times when it is especially important. Some of these situations are:

1. When the message is long or complicated
2. If the message seems unclear and could have more than one meaning (such as "meet me soon")
3. Any time you are receiving instructions
4. If you are having a negative response to something someone has said

To reword information, simply state in your own words what the other person's words mean to you. For example, suppose John says:

"I'm having a terrible week at work."

You realize "terrible week" could have many meanings. To verify, you might ask:

"You mean you're behind schedule?"

At this point, John can agree or say what he meant to say:

"No, but I mixed up two important orders."

Direct Questions: Another Method for Getting Information

You may wonder why not just ask a simple direct question, such as "Why?" or "What's wrong?" *Who, what, where, why* questions are still appropriate to use, but they can cause some people to feel under attack, and you may not get the detailed information you need. Remember when you were a teenager and a conversation like this took place?

Parent: Where did you go?

You: Out.

Parent: What did you do?

You: Nothing.

Or perhaps a conversation with a supervisor sounded like this:

Office manager: This job isn't done right.

You: What's wrong?

Office manager: You figure it out.

A conversation like the last one could be more productive if you seek to clarify and get detailed information more quickly about what is wrong, by using **verifying questions**. With this type of question, you reword what you believe the person means and state it as a question.

Office manager: This job isn't done right.

You: Is it the color or the size that's wrong?

Office manager: It's the color.

Verifying questions help you get to the meaning rapidly without wasting time guessing.

Direct questions can be useful when you need information from someone who is giving you instructions. Here is an example of using direct questions about instructions:

General contractor: Bring me the blueprints.

Carpenter: Where are they?

General: On the shelf.

Carpenter: What shelf?

General: The shelf by the door.

Carpenter: What door?

General: I'm in a hurry, just go look for them.

Direct questions can be unproductive and frustrating for both of you. Asking verifying questions that require yes-or-no answers, on the other hand, can help you gain information quickly and narrow the options in order to get specific information more rapidly. This communication tool is one way to find the detailed information you need without sounding like a lawyer conducting an interrogation.

Here is an example of using verifying questions about the same instructions:

General contractor: Bring me the blueprints.

Carpenter: Are they in the pickup?

General: No, they are on the shelf.

Carpenter: The shelf by the kitchen door?

General: No, the one in the bedroom.

Learning to use this tool takes effort and practice until you become comfortable, but the results are worth the time you spend. You will understand people better, with less frustration.

TOOLS OF COMMUNICATION

Getting Information, Part A

Instructions: Complete the two following situations with a partner using **direct questions** and **rewording questions.** Share your results with the class.

1. *Supervisor:* Get a different part for this machine.

<u>You (direct question):</u> _____

_____

<u>You (rewording):</u> _____

_____

2. *Supervisor:* I need you to work late today.

<u>You (direct question):</u> _____

_____

<u>You (rewording):</u> _____

_____

Getting Information, Part B

Instructions: For the statements in 1 and 2, use verifying questions to check the meaning. Imagine the customer or instructor's response to your question. Then compare your answers with the class. A variety of interpretations can be correct.

1. *Customer:* This equipment isn't running right!

Service rep: _____

_____

_____

Customer: _____

_____

_____

2. *Instructor:* Your diagram is inaccurate. I'd like you to do it over.

Service rep: _____

_____

_____

Customer: _____

_____

_____

Getting Information, Part C

Instructions: For 1, complete the exchange using verifying questions. For 2, develop your own dialog in which you use verifying questions to check facts.

1. *Helen* (with a *downcast expression*): I'd looked forward to my vacation, but now I don't know what to do.

You: _____

_____.

Helen: _____

_____

2. Write a short situation of your own:

_____

_____

_____

_____

_____

_____

Getting Information, Part D

Instructions: This exercise (Roach, unpublished) illustrates the skill of verifying information for electrical maintenance technicians. You can adapt it to your own career by substituting the terminology in your field. Look at the example, then complete the rest on your own.

Supervisor: I want a transformer bank tied so that I have 208/120 volts.

Employee: O.K., you want that transformer tied on a delta connection?

Supervisor: No, in a Y connection, O.K.?

1. *Jim:* I want you to put a service in.

Bill: _____

_____

Jim: _____

_____

2. *Instructor:* Your schematic is inaccurate, Alex. I'd like you to do it over.

Alex: _____

_____

Instructor: _____

_____

3. *Steve:* I would like to have you look at the main turbine motor.

Ed: _____

_____

Steve: _____

_____

4. *Bob:* John should never have gone into the field.

Don: _____

_____

Bob: _____

_____

5. *Judy:* I would like you to hook up a boiler feedpump.

Mike: _____

_____

Judy: _____

_____

4.5 COMMUNICATION BARRIERS

Barriers to communication sometimes interrupt the communication process, causing a break in the flow of information. The following are a few of those barriers.

Language: Words with multiple meanings often cause great confusion in the mind of the person receiving the message. Just think how many different definitions exist for the simple word *bar*—candy bar, salad bar, legal bar, ballet bar, metal bar! How many different meanings for *rock* can you think of? When a supervisor orders you to get your work done "soon," does he or she mean within minutes, an hour, or sometime this week?

Social: Thinking someone is above or beneath your social status can hinder honest communication. You may communicate quite differently with a coworker on the line than you would with a supervisor in the office.

Emotional: Being angry, upset, or even looking forward to payday can cause a person to be distracted, thus stopping the flow of communication.

Physical: Distracting noises or a personal hearing loss may contribute to a failure of communication.

Listening: As discussed previously, most people listen at only 25 percent efficiency. Improving listening and feedback skills is crucial to **getting the job** and **being successful on the job.**

Cultural differences: In today's global economy, cultural understanding is essential for a communication environment without barriers. We tend to judge others by our own standards, so we sometimes think people who are different are "weird" or wrong. Remember, *different* does not mean *deficient*. Diversity can bring an added positive point of view to the workplace. Since different cultures may have different values when relating to others at work, it will be helpful to have a general understanding of some of these differences.

TOOLS OF COMMUNICATION

Identifying Cultural Values

Instructions: Below are statements of beliefs and values of two very different cultures. Circle the number that best describes the cultural values with which you most closely identify.

CULTURE A				CULTURE B
	1	2	3	4

Task oriented: Focus on getting the job done. Work comes first, before family.

People oriented: Concern about the needs of workers. Family priorities come first.

	1	2	3	4

Linear thinking and working: Uses an orderly sequence of events. Finishes one step before going on to the next.

Nonlinear thinking and working: Typically works on and thinks about several projects at one time (e.g., being on the phone with a customer while filling out a request for department supplies at the same time).

	1	2	3	4

Direct conflict confrontation: A "get the cards on the table" or "What's wrong here?" attitude: "Let's talk about our problems."

Avoidance of direct conflict: Peace and harmony must be maintained at all costs. This approach to problem solving says, Perhaps a person could try this method." Conflict is avoided at all costs.

	1	2	3	4

Informal, casual communication style: Call the boss by his or her first name. Willing to discuss most of what's going on in life with almost anyone. "Everybody's a buddy."

Formal ways of speaking to others: Supervisors, older people, and even co-workers are spoken to formally ("Mr.," "Miss") until they are known well. Personal problems are not discussed at work. Few friendships are formed, and these are created slowly.

	1	2	3	4

Preference for working alone: Family includes only parents and children. Friendships are often of short duration.

Preference for working in groups: Family includes aunts, uncles, cousins. Close friends are viewed as brothers and sisters, and friendships are for a lifetime.

An awareness of some of your own communication barriers along with even a small degree of knowledge of cultural differences can assist you in the successful completion of communication transactions.

4.6   COMMUNICATION RULES

Communication rules can become barriers. We are usually taught these rules as children and often take them with us into our adult life. What were your early childhood communication rules? One rule around my own house was, "Don't interrupt anyone in authority." Another was "Don't yell at people, even if you're angry." On the other hand, in a large family the communication rule might be that *only* the *loudest* voice gets heard. You can imagine the problems that occur when someone from a "be quiet" family and an "only loudness wins" person work together on a team! Violations of personal communication rules can take place in the shop, office, or boardroom, causing a breakdown in the *communication circuit*.

4.7   THE "COMMUNICATION CIRCUIT"

Many people would define communication as writing, talking, or waiting to talk. However, there are two indispensable components of the communication circuit—*listening efficiently* and *providing accurate feedback*. Just as electricity cannot be delivered over a circuit if the connection is incomplete, neither can a spoken message be delivered if there are barriers to the completion of the communication circuit. These communication barriers can take the form of not listening or lack of feedback.

Understanding the complexity of the communication circuit can assist you in knowing how breakdowns occur. Once a breakdown is identified, it can be avoided or at least repaired. Communication breakdowns are often called "noise" or "static" since they interfere with an accurate understanding of a message. The causes of this noise are the six barriers to communication discussed previously:

Language	Physical
Social	Listening
Emotional	Cultural

WORLD OF WORK

Problem noises during a job interview develop while Joe is being interviewed by Sarah. He begins to talk negatively (his *message*) about the Barnes Company, his previous employer, and he uses poor eye contact (the *channel*). These two events cause Sarah (the *receiver*), who is interviewing him, to quit listening to him. She starts thinking about Joe's negative words and lack of eye contact.

Because of Sarah's not listening, she doesn't hear what he says later. Joe goes on to stress how he changed his original negative attitude toward the Barnes Company to a positive one. He also says he left there with excellent references, but Sarah hears none of this because she is not listening.

Because of her poor listening habits, she makes a snap judgment about Joe, classifying him as a negative person. She fails to ask any questions (get

(continued)

feedback) because she has decided *not* to hire him while she was *not* listening to what else he said.

A diagram of this dysfunctional communication circuit would look like this:

Noise
(Negative words)

1. Joe
(Sender)

2. Message
(Channels)

Noise
(No clarification)

5. Context
(Office noise)

Noise
(Poor eye contact)

3. Sarah
(Receiver)

4. Feedback
(None)

Noise
(Not listening)

We can find deeper causes for the "noises" in this interview. Joe was uncomfortable in an office setting because he had expected the interview to take place in the shop. In addition, he had never been interviewed by a woman. He found it very hard to concentrate in this situation, which probably accounted for his poor eye contact.

Because of the "noisy" communication circuit, Joe and Sarah both lost. Joe lost out on an employment opportunity because of his poor eye contact and ineffective choice of words. Sarah lost a potentially productive employee because of her inefficient listening skills and lack of feedback.

Stress Less

Inadequate communication, talking too much, or being misunderstood can create stress in our lives. Relaxing is one way to reduce stress. Another method is to become more physically fit. Ideas for doing this were described in earlier chapters. A person can further reduce stress by:

- Reducing the intake of nicotine and alcohol
- Eating foods that are low in fat and high in fiber
- Reducing consumption of foods that are high in salt, sugar, and caffeine, such as coffee, cola drinks, chocolate, tea, candy, and ice cream
- Consuming more foods with a high fiber content, such as whole wheat products, broccoli, cauliflower, potatoes (with low-fat toppings), spinach, and lettuce

[Suggestions adapted from Deaconess Medical Center Cardiac Rehabilitation Center (Stress, 1988).]

4.8 APPLYING THE CONCEPTS

CASE STUDY

As team leader, you talked to a coworker about her poor work production. You told her that her attitude was good but her performance was weak and she needed to improve her production level. Later she told another team member that she got a really good performance evaluation. She went on to say she does not need to change the way she does her work because you gave her a very positive performance evaluation. In the process of listening to you, she filtered out anything negative you said to her. Her selective listening attitude is reported to you. In work teams, decide how you would handle this poor listening situation.

CHAPTER PROJECT

In teams of three to five people, develop an information-checking exercise focused on your area of training. When your team has completed the situation specific to your work setting, exchange your exercise with another team and complete your team's responses to their project. Share the results with the class.

DISCUSSION QUESTIONS

1. What problems have you encountered when telephoning businesses for any reason?
2. Which poor listening habits are the most annoying to you?
3. Which of the feedback skills do you prefer using, direct questions or verifying questions? Why?
4. Which of the barriers to communication do you believe create the greatest problems when doing business?

SUMMARY

This chapter provided you with opportunities to learn and practice:

- Effective employment searches using the telephone
- Efficient listening skills
- Productive feedback tools
- Overcoming barriers to communication, including cultural differences and "noise" in the communication circuit

Using these skills on a consistent basis will help you to improve customer relations and communication at work with supervisors and coworkers.

The Interview: Preparing Well & Doing Your Best

LEARNING OBJECTIVES

1. Understand what employers look for during an interview.

2. Understand the pre-interview process as well as interviewing dos and don'ts.

3. Become familiar with the structure of interviews.

4. Practice answering typical interview questions.

5. Practice asking productive questions of the interviewer.

6. Practice participating in screening as well as focused interviews and learn to evaluate them.

7. Know the importance of thank-you letters, and practice writing one to the interviewer(s).

8. Apply the concepts.

The lack of adequate planning for an interview is the greatest single fault in the interviewing process. Even if your resume and letter of application are effective enough to get you an interview, you can't sit back and take the attitude, "I've got it made." You need to know how to communicate your personal skills, abilities, and work history effectively during the interview.

The survey in Chapter 1 reported the communication skills applicants need to possess when interviewing for a job. Different employers often seek different attributes in a potential employee. However, all employers stressed the need to know yourself, to know your goals, and to be able to share that information with enthusiasm during the interview. This chapter will explain the pre-interview and interview processes, help you express yourself clearly and positively to a potential employer, and show you how to follow up the interview effectively.

WORLD OF WORK

What do employers like to hear about during a job interview? During a televised employment seminar, a panel of employers stressed which qualities they look for in job candidates:

John Dacquistas, engineer, stressed the need for potential employees to differentiate themselves from the norm. He said he prefers the presentation of portfolios rather than resumes during job interviews because interviewers can get a better picture of the type of work a potential employee is able to produce. He went on to say that he has hired people because of the quality of their portfolio.

Molly Preston of Pathology Associates said, "I receive about 100 resumes per week, and 25 percent are screened out, never to be called, because of spelling errors."

Ivan Bush, School District 81, appreciates those who show flexibility, believe in themselves, value diversity, and have done some type of volunteer work in the community.

(Employment Seminar, 1996)

5.1 PREPARING FOR THE INTERVIEW: REVIEW YOUR SELF-ANALYSIS

The employment interview is a formal conversation between two or more people. It is an opportunity to let the interviewer know why you are the best person for the job. Being successful in the employment interview takes time, effort, planning, and good time management. Be sure to review the attitude and interest analysis you completed in Chapter 1 in order to talk about yourself in an organized manner. Review the techniques for researching a company that were presented in Chapter 3, so you will ask appropriate questions of the interviewer. Now, let's focus on what occurs during productive interview preparation.

Before you move through the door of the interviewer's office or shop, you should:

- Know yourself and be able to talk about your:
  - Strengths and weaknesses
  - Employment background, including all the places you have worked
  - Education and specialized training.
  - Short- and long-range goals

- Know what you want from the job:
  - The type of work environment you prefer
  - Whether you would rather work alone or as part of a group
  - Your salary needs
  - Whether you are willing to move if you get the job

- Know the company by:
  - Finding out what the company produces or what services they provide
  - Walking through the offices or shops if possible, and being prepared to show interest by asking questions
  - Trying to talk to some employees. Don't disrupt the flow of work. If the information you discover is positive, quote the employees during the interview.

- Know the description of the position you are interviewing for:
  - What is the experience level needed for the position?
  - What training will you need to complete if you get the job?
  - How well do you match the job description?

TOOLS OF COMMUNICATION

Interview Checklist

Instructions: Ask another member of the class to be your partner. Audiotape each other as you review the following self-analysis. Play back the tape and discuss your answers. Which ones are most effective? How can the others be improved? Which areas need to be explained more completely?

CHECKLIST

Before each interview, respond to the following questions *out loud*.

- ☐ What are my interests?
- ☐ What are my short- and long-range career goals?
- ☐ What are my short- and long-range personal goals?
- ☐ What are my skills and assets?
- ☐ What are my strengths and weaknesses?

Use this checklist *every time* you prepare for an interview, no matter how many times you have been interviewed in the past. Information about your goals or about the company may have changed since the last time you interviewed.

WORLD OF WORK

What Else Could It Take?

It is important to know what else the interviewer will probably expect you to bring to the interview. For example, if you are a chef, it will be good to show the interviewer a portfolio of your recipes and menus, including photos of dishes you have prepared. If you developed special drawings and blueprints in your civil engineering program, take them with you. Proof of citizenship or eligibility to work in the United States is sometimes necessary. Review suggestions for constructing a portfolio in Chapter 2. Call the company before the interview to see what supplemental information will be useful to bring with you.

5.2 THE PRE-INTERVIEW PROCESS

No matter how many times you apply for a job, review this list each time to remind you of the important elements of the process.

1. Plan your job hunting:

   - Start the job search as soon as you know you will need to find a position.

   - Plan your job hunt as a full-time project. You work a 40-hour week for an employer, and you should work no less for yourself.

   - Once you start the job-finding campaign, do not allow yourself little vacations.

   - Apply early enough in the day to allow sufficient time for multiple interviews, tests, or other hiring procedures that may be required.

   - Learn everything you can about the company before you apply: size, products, types of clothing employees are expected to wear, average salary, and hiring practices and policies.

   - Know why you want to work for the firm.

   - Follow up job leads immediately.

   - If this company does not schedule appointments, find out the best time of day and the best day of the week to apply.

   - If you learn of a job opening late in the day, call to arrange an appointment for the next day. They might postpone a hiring decision until you are interviewed.

2. Allow extra time to get to the interview. You never know when a train at a railroad crossing or a traffic roadblock could cause you to miss a valuable interview.

3. Go to the interview alone. Others could distract you or the people who interview you.

4. Do not carry packages with you. They, too, can become an awkward distraction. Carrying packages might give the impression that you are more interested in going shopping than in obtaining the job.

5. Men who are applying for a business position should wear a suit, shirt, and tie. Women also can wear a suit or a dress with a jacket. Neutral colors, conservative shoes, and tailored accessories are considered proper in most interview situations.

6. Some companies will not expect you to wear a business suit if you are applying for technical employment such as fluid power, electronics, carpentry, or welding, but wear clothing appropriate to the job. If you would be making service calls for this company, slacks and a shirt or blouse and maybe a jacket would be appropriate. Be neat, clean, and well groomed, and plan ahead of time what to wear.

7. Things to take with you to the interview:

   - Your Social Security card
   - Driver's license
   - Military records
   - School names, addresses, years attended, and transcripts

- Two pens—one black ink, one blue ink
- Pencils
- Extra paper and a calculator
- Money for bus fare or a telephone call
- Completed generic application form from Chapter 3
- Extra copies of your resume
- Your portfolio to show the interviewer
- Possibly a CD-ROM of your Web page and portfolio to leave with the interviewer
- A notebook or a nice folder with pockets to hold your papers (helps you to be organized).

8. Take any tools you might need to demonstrate your specific skills. For example, if you apply for a welding job, take your leathers and slag hammers with you.

9. Some organizations now require not only drug testing but also your driving record as a condition for employment. Be prepared for these possibilities.

10. Some companies provide a fragrance-free environment and do not permit cologne or perfume. You may want to check on this situation prior to the interview.

5.3   INTERVIEW DOS AND DON'TS

DO

- Do arrive at least 20 minutes before the scheduled interview to fill out application forms.
- Do write neatly on all application forms.
- Do remove your hat and comb your hair before the interview.
- Do look, feel, and act enthusiastic.
- Do believe in yourself, what you are doing, your education, your abilities, the company, and the job.
- Do emphasize your productivity and the quality of your work.
- Do sell yourself—let the interviewer know why you would be an asset to the company.
- Do sit up straight in your chair and lean forward slightly.
- Do keep your feet flat on the floor or cross your legs at the ankles. (Crossing your legs at the knees makes it too easy to jiggle your foot when you are nervous.)
- Do maintain direct eye contact with the interviewer to show interest and honesty.

DON'T

- Don't sit down until you are invited to do so. Waiting to be seated shows respect.
- Don't smoke or drink coffee, even if they are offered. There is a chance you could spill the coffee. The offer of a cigarette could be a way of find-

ing out if you smoke when the company maintains a smokeless environment.

- Don't eat anything unless the interview is conducted during a meal. In this situation, order something light.
- Don't drink alcoholic beverages before or during the interview.
- Don't put tools, a portfolio, or other materials on the interviewer's desk unless asked to do so.
- Don't lean on the interviewer's desk. The desk is the interviewer's personal space, and you don't want to "invade" it.
- Don't look around the room while the interviewer is talking.

Additional important things to remember are:

- Write down the names and positions of all the people you meet. A pocket-sized (3 x 5) notebook is useful for this purpose.
- Use the interviewer's name when shaking hands, occasionally during the interview, and when leaving the room—for example, "I'm glad to meet you, Mrs. Owen," and "Thank you for your time, Mrs. Owen."
- Shake hands with both male and female interviewers, even if you are also a woman.
- Relax as you talk.
- Listen attentively to the interviewer instead of thinking about what you will say next.
- Reflect your energetic attitude in the way you walk into and out of the room, your pleasant facial expression, and your cheerful tone of voice.
- Sound enthusiastic. Employers say they want to interview people they can hear and who sound as if they will have enough energy to last the day!
- Reflect your eager attitude by choosing positive words.
- Be prepared to answer questions honestly and with more than a "yes" or "no."

5.4 TYPES OF INTERVIEWS

Depending on the nature of the job and the employer's preferred style of interviewing, you may encounter various types of interview formats. Regardless of the format, an important component of job interviews is to maintain direct eye contact with the interviewer. (This is true in the United States. Expectations vary in other countries.)

WORLD OF WORK

A highly qualified young woman from the Philippines applied several times for various office technology positions in the United States, but was not hired. When she followed up on these interviews, she discovered that her poor eye contact was the primary factor contributing to the rejection. After discussing this revelation with her instructor, she was able to adjust her eye contact to a more direct Western style of nonverbal communication, even though, as she observed, "My grandmother would consider me to be very disrespectful if I looked her directly in the eyes, and she would spank me!"

Most interviews can be classified into one of five formats:

One-on-one interviews: In a one-on-one interview, you meet with one person at the company. The interview may be conducted by a personnel director as a screening interview and may involve questions to determine how well you fit into the company. It is often used by large companies such as the Boeing Corporation and Hewlett Packard. After this interview, the personnel director may *then* refer you to the business office or the technical area relevant to your training. You might be asked questions about your communication style or your problem-solving experiences, or you may be asked to demonstrate your computer or math skills.

- **Traits to communicate** in a one-on-one screening interview:
  - The ability to work independently as well as the ability to be part of a team
  - The ability to solve problems
  - The ability to communicate effectively
- **Suggestion:** Be ready to discuss specific examples of these abilities from previous work experiences and recent education.

Technical interviews: The **technical interview** is usually conducted in a shop or on the line by a specialist in the field. You may be asked to explain schematics or diagrams. The interviewer may request that you demonstrate your skills with actual materials. For example, if you are a welder, you might be asked to show your ability to weld in several positions. Because you never know when you will encounter this type of interview, be sure to take your tools with you to all interviews.

- **Traits to communicate** in this type of interview are:
  - Honesty: If you don't know about something or can't solve the problem in the schematic, say so!
  - Staying calm under pressure. If you get confused at some point, back up and start over.
- **Suggestion:** Because employers often want to see how you will respond in an actual work setting, be willing to say "I don't know" rather than pretend you know an answer.

Team interviews: Team interviews are conducted by two to five people as a group. This type of interview may be done in person, or you might be involved in a telephone conference call. The conference call would connect you with several people sitting around a table and either taking turns asking questions or allowing one person to ask questions while the others listen and make notes. Team interviews also may be conducted sequentially. The interviewee will meet with two to five people, one right after the other.

Team interviews are frequently used by companies who have an established group in place and want to see how you will fit in with that team.

- **Traits to communicate,** as for the technical interview, are:
  - Honesty
  - Flexibility
- **Suggestion:** Be careful of over-talking and over-answering questions. Too much information can disrupt the timing of the interview.

Social interviews: Social interviews are held during lunch or breakfast, or in some other informal setting. The purpose is to let the employer get to know the "real you" in a relaxed setting. The social interview may be the last in a series of interviews, but could be the first depending on the company and type of job. This style of interviewing is sometimes used by companies looking for people who will need to have social contact with potential and present customers.

- **Traits to communicate:**
  - **The ability to demonstrate effective customer relations** is essential. Give examples of how you calmed an irate customer or sold a product if that is part of your experience.

- **Suggestions:** Because this type of interview is often used to determine how well you fit socially within the work group, it is important to remember that although this is a social situation, it is still an interview! Be friendly and outgoing, but do not speak or act unprofessionally at any time. Dress appropriately. If you are not sure what to wear, wear the most conservative option you are considering. Order a light meal. Stick to nonalcoholic beverages.

Office or shop interviews: The **office or shop interview** is usually conducted by the office manager, line supervisor, or shop foreman to see how much you know about the company and the type of work they do. These interviews usually involve touring the office or shop with the interviewer, observing operations, and asking questions. You may also be asked to demonstrate your problem-solving skills in an unfamiliar environment.

- **Traits to communicate** in this situation are:
  - Your knowledge of the company
  - Interest in the operations, expressed by making observations and asking thoughtful questions

- **Suggestions:** Maintain a professional attitude by being positive about the company while avoiding being overly critical of their competitors.

WORLD OF WORK

Alternative Interviewing: When a Kansas native was prospecting for a better job, he went to a recruiting agency in Kansas City. Their procedure was to have him answer four questions that were recorded with a small video camera and to film a two-minute video in which he promoted himself. That video became part of his resume package. The video was seen by a company needing his skills, so they called him for an interview and hired him within days (Stafford, 2000).

Be prepared for more than one type of interview. People in many career areas will first have a personnel screening interview, followed by a technical, office, or shop interview. However, three or four interviews may be conducted before a hiring decision is made and depending on the responsibility level of the position.

TOOLS OF COMMUNICATION

Personal Skills

Instructions: Pick your strongest skill or the personal attribute you most want to emphasize during your next job interview. Think of specific examples of situations in which you demonstrated this skill. Describe how you might discuss it in the following interview formats:

Screening Interview: How could you emphasize your skill in problem solving when working with customers or coworkers? Give specific examples.

_____

_____

_____

_____

Office or Technical Interview: How could you emphasize your problem-solving skill in a work-related situation? Give specific examples.

_____

_____

_____

_____

5.5 INTERVIEW STRUCTURE

The interview style combined with the different types of questions form the overall structure of the interview. Most interviews contain four basic parts: the *opening, introduction, body,* and *closing.* This type of interview usually takes 30 to 40 minutes.

Opening

The opening of the interview involves greeting and getting acquainted. You and the interviewer become comfortable with each other. Remember that hiring decisions are often made during the first 90 seconds of an interview, and 30 to 70 percent of those decisions are based on nonverbal communication! Pay attention to your handshake, eye contact, and even how you walk and sit. Do not be too relaxed, but do not perch like a bird on the edge of your chair.

Time:	30 seconds to 2 minutes
Purpose:	To break the ice, become comfortable with each other.
Possible content:	Interviewer will welcome you and ask you to sit down. You will exchange names, chat informally about the weather, and so on.

Introduction

During the introduction, the interviewer explains the position and the company. He or she usually mentions the topics that will be discussed, when the hiring decision will be made, and the requirements for the job. Be sure to listen carefully so you do not ask questions later about something that was explained in the introduction. This would be a good time to mention your portfolio if you have brought one.

Time:	1 to 3 minutes
Purpose:	To give you basic information about the interview.
Possible content:	Brief overview of the company, positions available, ground rules for the interview.

Body

The body of the interview involves three parts: *exploration, your questions,* and *next steps.*

Exploration: First, the interviewer will explore your background, personal strengths and weaknesses, knowledge of the position and of the organization, and values and priorities that could affect your work. The interviewer wants to know about factors that will influence your job satisfaction. The employer also wants to be assured you are really willing to work, not just show up.

Time:	10 to 20 minutes
Purpose:	To identify your values, education, experience, and priorities relating to job performance.
	To compare your assets with the demands of the job.
	To see if you have a realistic view of the position and the company.
	To determine your level of self-knowledge.
	To predict your success as an employee.
Possible content:	Grades, internships, activities, coursework, and work experience.
	Types of problems you have encountered and how they were solved.
	Job qualifications and interest in the company.
	Your goals.
	Factors affecting your job satisfaction.
	Your ethics and personal values.

WORLD OF WORK

When discussing personal values and priorities, do not tell an interviewer what one carpentry student said: "I would rather do framing than finish work because I can hide my mistakes."

Your questions: The interviewer will usually ask if you have any questions. Be sure to have some prepared (later in this chapter you will find a list of questions to ask during an interview).

Time:	1 to 2 minutes
Purpose:	To give you a chance to learn information that has not been covered and to clarify any concerns that may have occurred to you during the interview.
Possible content:	Your questions should relate to the job description and job priorities, but not to money or benefits, unless you have been offered the position. You should already know about the salary and benefits because of the company research you conducted prior to the interview.

Identifying next steps: Finally, the interviewer will probably tell you what to expect next in the interviewing process. For example, the interviewer may tell you whether you will be called or if you should telephone for the results of the interview. Make sure to ask about the decision-making process if the interviewer does not give you this information.

Time:	1 to 2 minutes
Purpose:	To inform you of the next steps in the interview process or to offer you a position.
Possible content:	The interviewer will state how and when the company will contact you. The interviewer may ask you to call back at a certain time. Be sure to make notes so you can write an appropriate thank-you letter.

WORLD OF WORK

Be diplomatic when you clarify the final steps of your interviewing process. Saying "I want to work for your company" is appropriate. But saying, "My goal is to sit where you are sitting!" was viewed by one interviewer as being too aggressive. Remember, your purpose for the interview is to obtain a job offer; whether or not you decide to accept it is another issue. Another interviewer said the question "How soon can I start?" was too pushy. A way to inquire about the next steps politely could be, "When will you make your hiring decision?"

Closing

When the interview is over, always shake hands and thank the interviewer for his or her time, even if you do not think the interview was successful. Make sure to leave promptly when you sense that the interview is over.

Time:	30 seconds
Purpose:	To end the interview pleasantly and promptly.
Possible content:	The interviewer may put your resume aside, look at the clock, stand up, or say "Thank you for coming." This is your cue to thank him or her, shake hands, and leave.

The preceding format is the basic outline for an interview. A good interviewer will move through each of these stages with ease. A poor interviewer may get stuck or lost in one of the stages. If this happens, you may have to take some initiative and tactfully redirect the discussion.

5.6 ANSWERING INTERVIEW QUESTIONS EFFECTIVELY

Prior to the interview, it's a good idea to practice answering many different types of questions aloud. Watch yourself in the mirror and listen to yourself on audiotape. If possible, have someone videotape you in a practice interview so you can evaluate the total impression you make. Ask others to evaluate how you come across by using the interview evaluation forms provided later in this chapter. The more you practice answering questions, the more confident you will feel during the actual interview.

Most interviewers have a set of standard questions, but not all interviewers are trained in effective interviewing. Therefore, you need to know how to respond to vague or even illegal questions. You also will need to answer difficult questions about your background with honesty and confidence and be prepared to explain how you have overcome any past difficulties.

Answering Standard Interview Questions

Open-Ended Questions

When using this type of question, interviewers expect you to organize your thoughts and give them detailed information on a variety of topics. An example of an open-ended question is: "Tell me about your training." Practice how you will respond to open-ended questions by providing specific information highlighting those skills and experiences that make you the best candidate for the job. For example:

Interviewer: Tell me about your work experience.

Efficient response: I started working on the family farm while I was still in high school and learned to repair and operate the equipment in all types of weather, because when the crops are ready to harvest you don't take the day off. Since I've been in school, I'm working part time to help the instructor in his own machine shop on weekends and in the evenings.

Inefficient response: I worked on the family farm and part time while I'm in school.

Sometimes customer-relations problems may be stated in open-ended questions. For example:

Interviewer: What would you say if a customer comes in and demands that you work on his computer project immediately, but you are already working on another job?

Efficient response: "I'll be glad to help you when I finish this job I'm working on right now. That will probably be in about an hour. Do you want to wait and have a cup of coffee, or do you want to come back later? I can call your office when I'm ready for your project."

Inefficient response: "I'm busy, you'll have to wait your turn."

Be prepared for technical or problem-solving open-ended questions that are specific to your specialized training. For example:

Interviewer: Please show me (while displaying a schematic) where the problem is in this diagram.

Efficient response: I can trace the problem to here, but I'm not sure where to go next.

Inefficient response: The person who drew this diagram must have made a mistake. No circuit should be designed like this.

Being honest about what you know and don't know is much preferred to bluffing your way through the problem-solving process.

Closed Questions

Closed questions generally can be answered with one or two words. An example of a closed question is, "Did you like your previous job?"

To give the interviewer a better understanding of your abilities, you need to expand your answer rather than using just one or two words. It takes time and practice to learn how to answer closed questions with more than a yes-or-no answer. For example:

Interviewer: Did you like your last job?

Efficient response: Yes, I enjoyed the people I worked with at Smith Company, as well as the challenges of finding ways to solve the customers' problems.

Inefficient response: Yes.

Always use actual examples of how you accomplished a task or demonstrated a skill. This type of response will give the interviewer a more complete picture of who you are than a simple yes-or-no answer.

Rewording Vague Questions

The listening tools discussed in Chapter 4 are essential skills to use during job interviews. Some employers are not experienced interviewers, and their questions can be vague or general. The key is to clarify the vague question. For example:

Interviewer: Tell me, Susan, what do you like to do?

Efficient response: I have several interests, Mr. Jones. Would you like to know about my problem-solving efforts at work or about my hobbies?

Inefficient response: What do you mean?

The efficient response rewords the interviewer's question, is more detailed, and helps the interviewer focus on the information he or she really wants to know. When the interviewee phrases the answer in the form of a clarifying question, the interviewer is still in control of the situation. The inefficient response could put the interviewer on the spot and make him or her feel defensive.

TOOLS OF COMMUNICATION

Rewording Questions to Your Advantage

Instructions: Work with a partner. Take turns as interviewer and interviewee to practice clarifying open-ended questions quickly and efficiently. Audio- or video-tape each other, if possible. If you have difficulty wording your responses, write them out and then practice them out loud.

If you are working on this without a partner, you can still follow the same procedure. In this situation, audio- or videotaping your responses will be especially useful because you can see and hear how others might perceive you.

1. **Interviewer:** What have you done that shows initiative?

   Your response: _____

   _____

2. **Interviewer:** How do you define success?

   Your response: _____

   _____

3. **Interviewer:** What are your goals?

   Your response: _____

   _____

Redirecting Irrelevant or Illegal Questions

Another tool for answering questions successfully is **redirecting.** This technique is especially useful if an employer rambles on about irrelevant topics or asks illegal questions. Redirecting a question involves carefully and diplomatically turning the question away from the irrelevant or illegal topic and rephrasing it to highlight your skills. The goal is not to take control away from the interviewer, but to keep the focus on why you are the best person for the job.

Irrelevant Questions

The following question has nothing to do with the job:

> **Interviewer:** Ron, I see you're from the Northwest. I just read a book about Alaska. Have you ever been there?
>
> **Efficient response:** Yes, it's wonderful. I enjoyed going there with my family three years ago during a vacation. This gave me time to evaluate my priorities and set some employment goals. In fact, that's when I decided to get some advanced computer training, including the use of the machines like the ones you have here in the office.
>
> **Inefficient response:** Yeah, I went there with my family.

Note that even an irrelevant question can be used to introduce information about job-related skills!

Illegal Questions

According to the Federal Equal Employment Opportunity Act, most questions about religion, marital status, children, age, place of birth, race, and ethnic background are **not legal** during an interview. If you are asked a question about one of these topics, you may answer it if you choose to do so. However, another option is to redirect the questions by asking how that information would affect your ability to perform this job. If the employer does have valid reasons for asking this type of question, offer a short, focused answer. If the question is asked with a hidden motive or simply out of curiosity, redirecting the question will probably cause the interviewer to drop the topic. See Chapter 3 for a list of illegal questions.

Redirecting can be an effective way to respond to an illegal question. For example:

> **Interviewer:** Sally, I see on your application that you have two children. Who's going to take care of the children while you're at work?
>
> **Efficient response:** I have made child care arrangements. The children will not affect my availability to work, even to work overtime when necessary. In fact, during the two years I was getting my training I never missed a class because of problems with child care.
>
> **Inefficient response:** That's none of your business!

TOOLS OF COMMUNICATION

Redirecting Questions

Instructions: Practice redirecting questions by writing your responses to these questions. Share your ideas with the class.

1. **Interviewer:** What did you think about your training? *(vague)*

   <u>Your response:</u> _____

   _____

2. **Interviewer:** How old are you? *(This is usually illegal unless you would be serving liquor or for insurance purposes.)*

   <u>Your response:</u> _____

   _____

3. **Interviewer:** What nationality is your name? *(This is illegal.)*

   <u>Your response:</u> _____

   _____

Answering Difficult Questions

Difficult questions include questions about employment gaps in your resume, frequent job changes, time spent in jail, or lack of much work experience. Take the initiative to talk about difficult questions in a straightforward manner.

Here are several other difficult questions and sample responses.

Interviewer: Have you ever been convicted of a felony?

Efficient response: Yes, but I was younger [state how old you were if that is relevant], and actually this turned out for the best. I faced the results of my bad choices and turned my life in a positive direction by going back to school.

Inefficient response: Yes [with no explanation].

Interviewer: Have you ever been injured?

Efficient response: Yes, but since I've been cross-trained, I haven't had a problem with attendance at my technical training.

or

I was, but since then I have chosen a different career and I have experienced no physical limitations.

Inefficient response: Yes, I had a back injury when I worked at the mill.

Interviewer: You are retiring from the military. You must only want a part-time position.

Efficient response: Absolutely not! I am looking forward to the challenge of a career change and will enjoy this opportunity to develop another part of my life.

Inefficient response: Yes, I put in my twenty years.

TOOLS OF COMMUNICATION

Difficult Questions

Instructions: Practice answering difficult questions. Make your answers honest, straightforward, and positive. Work with a partner and take turns in each role. Audio- or videotape yourself if possible. If you have difficulty wording your responses, write them first, and then practice them out loud.

1. **Interviewer:** Why did you leave your last job?

   Your response: _____

   _____

2. **Interviewer:** What kind of a person annoys you?

   Your response: _____

   _____

3. **Interviewer:** What part of your technical training would you change?

   Your response: _____

   _____

Be cautious when expressing criticism. Criticism of a former employer or instructor during a job interview usually indicates a negative attitude on your part, and most employers do not want to hire someone with a negative attitude. When you are asked why you left a job, state your answer calmly, briefly, and truthfully. For example, "I left my previous position because I no longer felt that my responsibilities provided the challenges that I look for in a job." Do not say, "The boss was a jerk!" or "I didn't get along with my instructor."

5.7   ASKING PRODUCTIVE QUESTIONS

WORLD OF WORK

Linn Fyhrie, a line supervisor for Agilent, states that when a potential employee asks specific questions about the objectives and needs of his company, it is a positive factor in the interviewee's favor.

It is always productive to form questions demonstrating interest in and knowledge of the company where you are applying. Different types of questions are appropriate at different times during the interviewing process.

QUESTIONS TO ASK BEFORE YOU ARE OFFERED THE JOB

- Do you have an education/training program? Please describe it.
- What specific responsibilities are trainees given?
- What percentage of your leadership openings are filled from within?
- Did my resume raise any questions that I can answer?
- Are there some negative aspects to the job you are offering?
- Would you please describe the duties (or responsibilities) of the job (if they have not been explained)?
- Was the person who previously held this job promoted?
- Could you please tell me about the people I would be working with?
- What is the single largest problem facing your department [staff or crew] now?
- Will there be an opportunity for advancement?
- What personal tools would be required for this job?
- How often are employees evaluated? At what intervals are written performance evaluations given?

QUESTIONS TO ASK AFTER THE EMPLOYER HAS OFFERED YOU THE JOB

- Could you please tell me about the benefits of the company? (You really should have investigated and should know this information before applying for the job.)
- Are there investment options?
- What's the cost of living and the housing situation where I'd be employed? (if you are moving to another area)

QUESTIONS TO ASK IF YOU DON'T GET THE JOB

- Are there others in the organization who might be interested in someone with my qualifications and experience?
- Do you know of another company that is looking for someone with my skills?
- Do you have any suggestions for improving my resume or interviewing skills for my next interview?

QUESTIONS TO ASK IF THE INTERVIEWER IS UNDECIDED

- When will a decision be made?
- May I call you later in the week? (depending on the response to the previous question)
- What time or day would be convenient for me to call?

TOOLS OF COMMUNICATION

What Do You Want to Know?

Instructions: Develop a list of five additional questions that you would like to ask the interviewer at your next job interview, such as:

- What additional computer skills would you suggest for this position?
- What "people" skills will someone in this position need to use?
- Do you foresee any reorganization in your company in the near future?

1. _____
2. _____
3. _____
4. _____
5. _____

The next exercise provides experience in a critical phase of the employment process. Even if you have been interviewed dozens of times, try this exercise to further sharpen your communication tools.

TOOLS OF COMMUNICATION

Screening Interview

Instructions: A short, structured interview is often used by personnel departments when screening applicants for various departments. It usually takes 10 or 15 minutes.

1. Visualize a specific company you would like to work for, write a job description that would be applicable to your field of study, and select 8 to 10 of the questions listed on page 140.

2. Work with a partner and interview each other using the outlines you just developed. Audiotape your responses or, preferably, videotape this practice interview.

3. Now, play back the tape. Evaluate each other and yourselves according to the rating sheet below.

4. Compare your evaluations. What are your strengths? How could you improve your answers the next time? Did your answers give specific examples of work you have done?

Most responses should be a minute or two in length. Do not over-talk and bore the interviewer or try to take control of the interview.

If you are working alone, ask the questions of yourself and answer them out loud while you audiotape yourself. Then play back the tape and evaluate yourself. Alternatively, write out your answers in the space provided to get a visual picture of what you want to say.

ANSWERING INTERVIEW QUESTIONS

Interviewee: _____

Your name: _____

Answers rated **excellent** will be detailed, with job-specific examples.
Answers rated **good** will involve less detail and fewer examples.
Answers rated **fair** will be shorter and have only one or two examples.
Answers rated **poor** will be primarily yes-or-no answers and contain no specific examples.

	[2] POOR	[3] FAIR	[4] GOOD	[5] EXCELLENT
1. WORDING THE ANSWER:				
Used complete sentences	■	■	■	☐
Positive answer	■	■	■	☐
Was specific	■	■	■	☐
2. NONVERBAL MESSAGE:				
Posture	■	■	■	☐
Facial expressions	■	■	■	☐
Eye contact	■	■	■	☐
Hands and gestures	■	■	■	☐
Legs and feet	■	■	■	☐
3. VOICE:				
Volume	■	■	■	☐
Interest and enthusiasm	■	■	■	☐
Sounded positive	■	■	■	☐
Energy level	■	■	■	☐
TOTAL	☐	☐	☐	☐

Comments _____

_____

SCREENING INTERVIEW QUESTIONS

Interviewer's Introduction

The purpose of this interview is to gather data pertinent to an interest in employment that you may have with our company. As we proceed, we will not delve too much into the actual specifics of your skills or trade. That will be accomplished at a later interview. We are looking for information about you. Do you have any questions before we proceed?

1. What kind of work would you most like to do for our company?

2. Please describe any activities that have provided you with experiences, training, or skills that you feel will help you in the position you are applying for.

3. Are there certain activities you feel more confident performing than others? What are they and why do you feel that way?

4. Tell me about your last or present job, describing what you did, your major responsibilities, and your typical day. Of the responsibilities you mentioned, which presented the most difficulty for you?

5. What were some of the problems you encountered in performing your last job and how did you overcome them?

6. What is your real career objective? What have you done or intend to do outside of your job to help you reach this objective?

7. We are looking for employees with a commitment to this position. Are there any reasons why you might not stay with us?

8. Do you have any commitments that would prevent you from working regular hours? Are you available to work overtime, if needed? *(If yes:)* Are there any limitations or restrictions on your ability to work overtime?

9. Do you have any health conditions that would prevent you from performing all the duties of this job?

10. What was your absentee record at your prior place of employment or at school?

11. Do you anticipate missing workdays because of any health condition?

12. What is your strongest personal quality or qualification? Why?

13. What is your weakest personal quality or qualification? Why?

14. What specific job factors are important to you?

15. What job factors would you like to avoid in a job? Why?

16. Are there any other factors that we have not discussed that make you uniquely qualified for this position?

(Structured Screening Interview Format developed by John Goetz, Human Resources Department, Community Colleges of Spokane, Spokane, WA. Used by permission.)

Now you are ready for a more focused type of interview.

TOOLS OF COMMUNICATION

Interviewing in Teams

Instructions: Work in teams of three to five people. Use the format for the detailed interview on pages 127–131, and choose 12–15 questions that appear below. Develop an outline for an interview for your technical field. Conduct an interview for each member of the team. Audiotape the interview or, preferably, videotape it. Evaluate the nonverbal communication, and note appropriate answers and areas that still need improvement. Be sure everyone has an opportunity to be both an interviewer and an interviewee. One team member can operate the video equipment, while other team members will be the evaluators, using the second evaluation form on page 141.

This exercise can be conducted in front of the entire class or used as a team project. The instructor also may evaluate the in-class demonstration or the tapes and provide individual feedback.

If you are working alone, write out your answers to the following questions. Then audio or videotape your responses, play them back, and evaluate yourself. You could also benefit from having a friend, fellow student, or coworker evaluate your tape and offer feedback about your interviewing strengths and weaknesses.

TEAM INTERVIEW QUESTIONS

1. What are your future plans in this technical field?
2. How do you spend your spare time? What are your hobbies?
3. In what type of position are you most interested?
4. Why do you think you might like to work for our company?
5. What jobs have you held? How did you obtain them? Why did you leave?
6. What courses did you like best? Least? Why?
7. Why did you choose your particular field of work?
8. What do you know about our company?
9. Do you feel that you have received a good general training?
10. What qualifications do you have that make you feel that you could be successful in your field?
11. What are your ideas on salary?
12. If you were starting your training all over again, what courses would you take?
13. Can you forget your education and start from scratch?
14. Do you prefer any specific geographic location? Why?
15. Why did you decide to go to this particular school?
16. What do you think determines a person's progress in a good company?
17. What personal characteristics are necessary for success in your chosen field?
18. Why do you think you would like this particular type of job?
19. Do you prefer working with others or by yourself?
20. What kind of boss do you prefer?
21. Can you take instructions without feeling upset?
22. Tell me about an experience that has affected your life.

23. How did previous employers treat you?

24. What have you learned from some of the jobs you have held?

25. Can you get recommendations from previous employers?

26. What interests you about our product or service?

27. Since this job creates a lot of stress, what do you do to reduce stress?

28. Have you ever changed your major field of interest while in college? Why?

29. Do you feel you have done the best scholastic work of which you are capable?

30. What do you know about opportunities in the field for which you are trained?

31. How long do you expect to work for us?

32. Have you ever had any difficulty getting along with fellow students or faculty?

33. What are your plans for furthering your education?

34. Do you like routine work?

35. Do you like regular hours?

36. Define *cooperation* and give an example of when you demonstrated this quality.

37. Will you fight to get ahead?

38. Do you have an analytical mind?

39. Are you eager to please?

40. Have you had any serious illness or injury?

41. What job in our company would you choose if you were entirely free to do so?

42. Is it an effort for you to be tolerant of persons with a background or interests different from your own? Give an example of how you worked out those differences.

43. What types of people seem to "rub you the wrong way"?

44. What jobs have you enjoyed the most? Least? Why?

45. What are your own special abilities?

46. Would you prefer a large or a small company? Why?

47. What is your idea of how this industry operates today?

48. Do you like to travel?

49. How about overtime work?

50. What are the disadvantages of your chosen field?

51. Do you think that grades should be considered by employers? Why or why not?

52. Are you interested in research?

53. What have you done that shows initiative and willingness to work?

Note: When you are preparing for an interview, if you will take the time necessary to write out brief answers to each of the questions in this list, it will help you to clarify your own thinking and establish ready answers.

(Adapted from *Job Finding Kit,* published by the Coordinating Council for Occupational Education.)

INTERVIEW EVALUATION FORM

Evaluator: _____

Interviewee: _____

Date: _____

	POOR [2]	FAIR [3]	GOOD [4]	EXCELLENT [5]
1. Opening	▣	▣	▣	☐
2. Describing background	▣	▣	▣	☐
▪ Tied in direct and indirect job-related experience to job description.	▣	▣	▣	☐
▪ Tied academic background to job opening.	▣	▣	▣	☐
3. Professional attitude	▣	▣	▣	☐
4. Interview preparation	▣	▣	▣	☐
▪ Knowledge of the company	▣	▣	▣	☐
▪ Knowledge of the position	▣	▣	▣	☐
5. Career objectives clear and realistic	▣	▣	▣	☐
6. Personal appearance	▣	▣	▣	☐
7. Self-confidence	▣	▣	▣	☐
▪ Believes in own ability.	▣	▣	▣	☐
▪ Is positive about self.	▣	▣	▣	☐
8. Positive verbal communication	▣	▣	▣	☐
▪ Answered questions quickly.	▣	▣	▣	☐
▪ Used overview statements, then developed specifics.	▣	▣	▣	☐
▪ Turned negative points into assets.	▣	▣	▣	☐
9. Positive nonverbal communication	▣	▣	▣	☐
10. Revealed dynamic personal energy	▣	▣	▣	☐
11. Overall rating for interview	▣	▣	▣	☐

TOOLS OF COMMUNICATION

Video Self-Analysis

Name: _____

This self-analysis is worth 25 points and is due on the day of your scheduled playback. Be sure to bring your videotape to the playback session.

Instructions: Watch your videotaped interview and evaluate it using the form on p. 141, then answer the following questions:

1. What did you like best about how you responded to the interviewer? Be specific.

_____

_____

_____

_____

_____

_____

_____

2. What did you like least about how you responded to the interviewing situation? Again, be specific.

_____

_____

_____

_____

_____

_____

_____

3. What specific changes would you make in your next interview?

_____

_____

_____

_____

_____

_____

_____

5.8   FOLLOWING UP WITH FLAIR

Congratulations! You made it through the interview! However, you cannot afford to sit back and relax while waiting for the phone to ring with the news that you got the job. You are now in the follow-up phase of the interviewing process. Interview follow-up is important to your success in getting a job because it provides one more opportunity to let employers know you are interested in their employment opportunity. Even if you do not want to work there, an expression of appreciation for the time spent with you will help to maintain your network of employers. The first thing you need to do in this follow-up process is to write a thank-you letter to the interviewer(s).

Thank-You Letters

Thank-you letters should be written on the same day as the interview, while you are still feeling enthusiastic and can remember details. Nervousness or mistakes made during the interview can also be discussed in a thank-you letter.

An effective thank-you letter will contain the following elements, but not necessarily in this order:

- An expression of your gratitude for the interview, including the date of the interview
- The position for which you were interviewed
- A reminder of two or three of your specific skills relating to the opening
- A summary statement of your interest in the job, including your telephone number
- A complimentary closing

If you are pressed for time, a handwritten note is acceptable, if your handwriting is legible. Be sure to include all the information that is suggested for the more formal business or computer-generated letter. Use plain, professional-looking stationery.

WORLD OF WORK

Thank-you letters are an important first thing to do in the follow-up process. One applicant took the time to thank the interviewer in writing even though she did not get the job she had applied for. When the newly hired employee was fired, the woman who had written the letter was offered the position. The employer said that she had demonstrated good attention to detail by taking the time to write the letter, and that attention to detail was a vital quality in this career.

Route 2, Box 104A
Cheney, WA 99004
May 27, 2001

Mr. Tom Neuman
Personnel Manager
Daytron Corporation
PO Box 14687
Spokane, WA 99214

Dear Mr. Neuman:

I would like you to know how much I appreciated being interviewed by you yesterday for the fluid power position.

I believe my background with the military, which included work in hydraulics, pneumatics, and management, in conjunction with training in Fluid Power Technology at Spokane Community College, has prepared me for the work we discussed. I am looking forward to being associated with Daytron Corporation in its growth as it develops the new plant in Cheney.

I will be contacting you June 15, as you requested, regarding employment with Daytron at the Cheney location. My message phone is 328-4250 if you need to talk to me before that date. Thank you, once again, for your time and consideration.

Sincerely yours,

Charles V. Hayord

Charles V. Hayord

CVH/bjr

FIGURE 5.2   *Thank-you letter including additional information and materials.*

4707 E. Upriver Dr. #W-103
Roseburg, OR 97470
November 20, 2001

Mr. John Mark
President
VSD Corporation
3650 East 3rd Avenue
Salem, Oregon 97301

Dear Mr. Mark:

Thank you for interviewing me yesterday for the technician position. I appreciated the opportunity to talk with you about the future of your company and I am looking forward to working with you after the first of the year and beyond.

I would like to address two points you asked during the interview. First, I appreciated your discernment in pointing out that I have had an unstable employment record. I assure you that if I am given this golden opportunity as I view it, I am committed to your company and have no intention of leaving. It is my earnest desire to grow with you and stay with you for the long haul. Second, you asked why my instructor Ed White was not on my list of references. Please feel free to contact him at (320) 533-7036. I worked for Ed as a work-study last year and we have an excellent relationship. It was also a pleasure to meet Matt Matthews. He was very kind and I appreciated his giving me a tour of your facilities. Please express my thanks to him as well.

I have enclosed some AutoCAD drawings that I completed as part of my coursework. I am confident that you will see they demonstrate my abilities with the technical drawings, and I would be happy to assist your salespeople in learning AutoCAD.

I look forward to talking with you in December regarding employment after January 1, 2002. I can be reached at (320) 487-3483 after 3:00 p.m. Thank you once again for your time and consideration.

Sincerely,

Austin Taylor

Austin Taylor

Enclosures

FIGURE 5.3   *Thank-you letter by an applicant who was not asked to call back.*

12702 East Hale
Greeley, CO 83815
December 14, 2002

Ms. Ester Boyd, Director
Human Resources
Nighthawk Corporation
2711 Brighton St.
Denver, CO 47836

Dear Ms. Boyd:

I appreciated the opportunity to talk with you December 12th about the computer programming position. The prospect of working with the Nighthawk Corporation is exciting. I was pleased that the problem-solving skills developed at the Coles Company and my education at Weld County Community College are so close to the qualifications you described.

It was also a pleasure for me to meet Mr. Fisher, who is in charge of the lab. The time he took to give me a tour of the lab was very helpful. Please express my thanks to him as well.

You may call (567) 928-0248 between 8:00 a.m. and 5:00 p.m. regarding this position. I will look forward to hearing from you.

Sincerely,

Charles B. Hibbert

Charles B. Hibbert

FIGURE 5.4   *Thank-you letter giving further information by an applicant who was not asked to call back.*

P.O. Box 1787
Dover, OH 44612
November 15, 2002

Mr. Frank Shell
Instructor
Stark Community College
2015 West High Ave.
New Philadelphia, Ohio 44663

Dear Mr. Shell:

I appreciate being interviewed by you November 9, 2002, for the heavy equipment supervisory position.

However, I did not elaborate on my early management and people skills. Before my twenty-first birthday, I was a non-commissioned officer in the U.S. Army, which put me in direct supervision of many personnel. I was also assigned to various Inspector General teams, which made me responsible for the thorough inspection of hundreds of pieces of construction equipment.

I believe my extensive background and education, combined with my people skills, have prepared me for the position we discussed.

You may call (330) 343-5687 between 5:00 a.m. and 2:30 p.m. regarding this position. I will look forward to hearing from you.

Sincerely,

Raymond L. Park

Raymond L. Park

TOOLS OF COMMUNICATION

Writing Thank-You Letters

Instructions:

1. Develop two "Thank you for the interview" letters addressed to someone who interviewed you, one for each of the following situations:

   a. You were asked to call back to find out the company's decision.

   b. You were not asked to call back, perhaps made a mistake, omitted vital information about your background, or were overly nervous.

2. Ask someone else who is trained in writing skills to evaluate your letters using the following rating form. This person could be a fellow student, instructor, or friend. Be certain the person has current and accurate knowledge of business letters.

3. After you receive feedback from someone else, revise and correct the letters and keep them in a folder for use following future job interviews.

RATING THE THANK-YOU LETTER

	POSSIBLE POINTS	YOUR LETTER
1. Thank-you statement	10	
2. Date of interview	10	
3. Name of position	10	
4. Statement of your skills related to the job, and/or clearing up any errors made during the interview	20	
5. Statement of interest in the job	10	
6. Your telephone number	10	
7. Complimentary closing	5	
8. Neatness and alignment	5	
9. Correct spelling, punctuation, and sentence structure	20	
TOTAL	100	

Follow-up Self-Analysis

Think about what you can do to improve your next interview. Analyze the questions you asked and the answers you gave at your last interview. Ask yourself:

- Did I have enough information about the company?
- Did my skills and abilities match the job description?
- Did I need to share more specific examples from previous work experiences?
- Did I talk too long or not long enough?

- Did I sound enthusiastic?
- Did I use effective nonverbal communication skills?

Follow Up by Keeping a Log

After an interview, it is helpful to keep a notebook of the dates of your interviews, including the names and positions of anyone you spoke to. This is especially important for future correspondence. Remember to keep all job information confidential until you get the job. You may create unnecessary competition for yourself by discussing the job opening with others.

Writing another follow-up letter a week or two after your first thank-you letter will demonstrate your continued interest in the job. Even if the position is filled by someone else, you never know when another opportunity with that employer may occur.

Some employers may prefer a thank you by e-mail, so check to see the expectations of the interviewer.

Finally, don't stop looking for work while you wait for an answer from one company. Keep looking for employment with other companies until you receive a job offer!

Whether you are chosen for the job or not, remain confident, positive, and enthusiastic. Know that soon you will be hired for a job that's right for you!

WORLD OF WORK

An article in *USA Today* described a survey conducted by Robert Half (1989), president of the research firm Robert Half International. He surveyed 100 personnel directors to find out the kinds of crazy things people do and say during job interviews.

Here are some examples:

"Dozed off and started snoring during the interview."

"Wore a Walkman and said she could listen to me and the music at the same time."

"Interrupted to phone his therapist for advice on answering specific interview questions."

"Brought her large dog to the interview."

"Stretched out on the floor to fill out the job application."

The most important thing to do during a job interview, Half says, is the easiest: *Be nice.* An interview is a tense situation, so *try to think of the word "smile."*

5.9 ACCEPTING AN OFFER

When you are offered the job, a few companies expect a letter of acceptance. Figure 5.5 provides an example of such a letter.

FIGURE 5.5   *Letter of acceptance.*

2002 Hollow Lane
Fresno, CA 98989
June 12, 2002

Frank Johnson
Timken Corporation
3015 Franklin Avenue
Canton, Ohio 44630

Dear Mr. Johnson:

Thank you for the offer of the position as civil engineer at your Stark plant. I accept the position and am eager to begin work.

I am prepared to begin work August 8, 2002, as you suggested in your e-mail. The terms and conditions of your offer are acceptable to me: $32.50 per hour for the first six months with increments to follow based on performance. I realize there is a requirement for a UA along with a physical prior to my being accepted in the health plan. I have already scheduled an appointment with your designated health care provider.

I appreciate this opportunity for employment and to be an asset to your team. I look forward to beginning work on August 8th.

Sincerely,

Tim Graham

Tim Graham

Stress Less

When you are looking for employment, you do not have the time to help every-one who needs your assistance, so you need to learn how to say no in a positive way. Try responding to requests this way: "I would really like to help you, but I have to get ready for a job interview. Maybe we can get together on Sunday afternoon."

This type of a response not only affirms your care for the person but also affirms your need to devote time to the job search.

5.10 APPLYING THE CONCEPTS

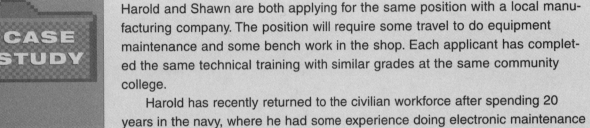

CASE STUDY

Harold and Shawn are both applying for the same position with a local manu-facturing company. The position will require some travel to do equipment maintenance and some bench work in the shop. Each applicant has complet-ed the same technical training with similar grades at the same community college.

Harold has recently returned to the civilian workforce after spending 20 years in the navy, where he had some experience doing electronic maintenance work aboard ships.

Shawn completed his technical training right after graduating from high school and held a part-time job for an auto parts store during high school and college.

Discuss this situation in small groups, and have someone record the group's answers. Share the observations later with the class. List each group's answers on the board.

1. What are Harold's strengths? His weaknesses?

2. What are Shawn's strengths? His weaknesses?

3. As a team, decide which one you would hire, and explain why.

DISCUSSION QUESTIONS

1. What questions would you want to include in a job interview if you were the employer?

2. Which type of interview do you think is the most valuable: one-on-one, technical team, social, office, or shop? Why?

3. How would you rate the importance of eye contact during a job interview on a scale of 1 to 5 (1 is low and 5 is high)? Why?

4. Which three questions do you believe are the most useful to ask a poten-tial employer?

SUMMARY

In this chapter you learned about:

- Self-analysis and self-evaluation forms for each phase of the pre-interview, interview, and follow-up process
- Factors employers consider important during job interviews
- Factors that can affect the job interview negatively
- Various interviewing formats
- Different types of interviewing questions
- Efficient and inefficient answers to questions
- A detailed screening interview
- Thank-you letters

Communicating Effectively with External Customers

LEARNING OBJECTIVES

1. Understand the differences between internal and external customers.

2. Learn how to remember customers' names.

3. Learn how to discover customers' wants and needs.

4. Discover how perception affects productive communication with customers.

5. Practice the skill of perception checking.

6. Practice communicating with customers on the phone.

7. Learn how to communicate with critical customers.

8. Understand some cultural differences.

9. Practice giving verbal sales, service, or technical reports.

Once you are employed, it is vital to focus on communicating effectively with customers. Customers may be either *external* or *internal*. **External customers** are those who receive the products or services and who do not work for the company. **Internal customers** are those who work *within* the company. Internal customers are more commonly known as your coworkers.

In his book *Customer Comes Second,* Hal Rosenbluth (1992) points out the need to maintain healthy communication within the business in order to preserve a productive environment. Smooth associations internally usually will achieve positive results externally.

This chapter discusses the specific communication tools most useful when communicating with external customers. Chapter 7 will provide some guidelines for working effectively with coworkers.

A survey in the year 2000 of 329 employers in the United States stressed the importance of customer relations. In fact, 65 percent of these employers said the one thing that could get an employee fired was the inability to get along with external customers. Employers place such importance on their employees' ability to get along with external customers because it dramatically affects the company's performance. According to previous research, when external customers quit doing business with a company, over half of them quit because of an indifferent attitude toward them by employees.

WORLD OF WORK

"In an amazing number of companies whose front-line workers have some interaction with customers, communication skill isn't a nice-to-have; it's a must-have," says AEA's Fields-Tyler. (Jacobs, 1996)

Good service is an important aspect of relating to external customers. Good service means:

- Knowing what the customer wants and needs
- Using the correct communication tools necessary to meet those needs and wants

6.1   WHAT DO CUSTOMERS WANT?

In general, external customers look for businesses that will give them prompt service and/or solve their problems. Providing what the customer is looking for starts with basic courtesy and understanding of who they are and what they need.

Who Is the Customer?

WORLD OF WORK

One thing that will help a customer to be comfortable is to be identified by the correct name. At an office, one customer was mistakenly called by the wrong name twice. *Two years* later, she was still telling others about the incompetence of the people in that office—just because someone spoke to her using an incorrect name!

From the customer's point of view, if you can't remember his or her name, how can you remember—and fulfill—his or her product or service requirements? A person's name is his or her badge of individuality. Using customers' names lets them know you are really interested in them.

Try using the following four points in order to remember names more easily.

1. *Be really interested.* You must *really want* to improve your ability to remember names before you will make any progress. As Dale Carnegie said, "The ability to remember names is not an inherited gift. It is just plain work plus the desire to 'want to'!"

2. *Form an impression.* It is important to get a clear impression of a name before you can hope to remember it. First, listen to the name carefully when you are being introduced. Ask to have the name repeated if you did not understand it. Then ask to have the name spelled, and write it down for a visual image. Second, get a vivid impression of the person. Note the facial and physical characteristics of the person. Get a distinct impression of the voice.

3. *Repeat.* You will have less trouble remembering a name if you repeat it often. Repeat the name right after hearing it, and use the customer's name several times during the conversation.

4. *Relate.* Form a connection between the person's face and the name with a mental picture, such as "Fred Small is tall." Or make a memorable association, such as "Ted Ford drives a Chevy." The association may be made by linking the name with what the person does: *Ron works at the "Bon."* You can also use rhyme: *Sally, alley.*

What Does the Customer Need?

Customers have more basic needs than just to feel good because someone knows their names. According to Abraham Maslow, the basic human needs are:

Air, water, food, physical well-being.   If customers come in while you are very busy, offer them a cup of coffee or tea so they will be more comfortable while waiting for you.

WORLD OF WORK   Many businesses offer complimentary beverages for customers who are waiting. A large eye clinic also has water, cookies, and candy available for its patients. Some places provide children's toys, crayons, and books for waiting clients and their children. In each of these examples, the employers make an organized effort to meet some basic needs of the external customer—the need for water, food, or physical comfort.

Safety.   The next basic need is to be safe. If customers want to "help" in the shop, it will be essential to stress the necessity of staying in safe areas, perhaps by painting "Don't Go Beyond This Line" on the shop floor. If this does not work, a partitioned waiting area with chairs, magazines, and newspapers can be developed to keep them safe.

Financial security.   Financial security is the next basic need. This need is especially important to consider in giving cost estimates to customers or clients. When you think the costs will exceed your original estimate, be sure to explain this information promptly. To retain your customers, do not let extra costs come as a surprise when the customers receive the bill! A surprise price increase will probably be the quickest way to cause them to go elsewhere with their business.

Friendship. Another basic human need is for friendship. It is important to maintain a level of friendship with your customers. This does not mean inviting them home for dinner, but it does mean treating them as individuals and not as strangers who happened to walk in off the street. This can be accomplished by remembering such things as their preferences in color, style, football teams, or food. Being able to talk with others about their particular choices is a way to deal with them as valued individuals rather than as just another number in the files.

Succeeding on the job and in life. Succeeding on the job is the final basic need. When others tell you about their employment promotions and successes, remember to congratulate them. This recognition can serve as one more method to maintain effective customer relations. It will be equally important to congratulate your coworkers on their achievements because you will be acknowledging their worth and value to the company (adapted from material quoted in Lamberton and Minor, 1995).

These five basic human needs must be fulfilled in the order they exist. It is difficult to talk to someone about financial security if that person is hungry, has no place to live, or believes the surroundings are unsafe. The first three needs usually must be fulfilled in the order of their priority before a person is truly able to focus on numbers four and five.

Considering the basic needs of human beings allows you to relate successfully to different types of customers. Sometimes customers may focus on one specific need and not progress through them in this orderly five-step process. Be prepared to accommodate this difference. For some people, financial security is much more important than feeling safe. These individuals will need detailed cost estimates, not a general idea, such as "around $100." Otherwise, they may feel cheated or taken advantage of and will take their business elsewhere.

In addition to knowing the importance of basic human needs, understanding **perceptual differences** will be a great advantage when communicating with customers and coworkers.

6.2   PERCEPTION

Webster's New World Dictionary (1986) defines the process of perception as "the mental grasp and interpretation of people, situations and objects by means of the five senses" (p. 1054). In communication, it means the way a person understands a situation or a statement—which may be different from yours.

Being able to understand the customer's perceptions is vital for successful communication.

WORLD OF WORK   Often, when dealing with customers and coworkers, there are differences in the perception of a situation. Customers may think you are ignoring them because you do not speak to them right away. They may think you don't care about their needs when you are just trying to finish a job that was due an hour ago.

Customers from other countries often will have very different ideas of the proper way to conduct business. They may expect to engage in some friendly conversations prior to doing business because from their point of view it is important to get to know a person before you can trust this person to be involved in any business transaction. But what if you are from the United States, have an appointment in five minutes, are very time conscious, and just want to find out what the customer from overseas wants so that you can get to your appointment on time? The customer's interpretation may be that you are unfriendly and rude, and that he cannot complete this undertaking with a stranger who takes so little time to become acquainted with customers. Your interpretation is that this person is wasting time because he will not get to the point about what he really wants, but keeps asking about your family. Misunderstanding the situation may cause each of you to lose money since you did not try to understand each other's point of view.

TOOLS OF COMMUNICATION

Cultural Expectations

Instructions: With a partner, brainstorm at least five ideas about how you could handle the preceding conflict of relating to a customer whose cultural expectation is that friendships are important versus getting to the point in order to go to your next appointment. Share your ideas with the class.

If you are working alone, how many ideas can you think of for solving this problem caused by a cultural misunderstanding?

Since no person can possibly anticipate every misunderstanding because of individual and cultural differences, it is helpful to use another communication tool: **perception checking.**

A *perception check* is useful when dealing with others in order to determine the correct understanding of their needs and expectations. Using this technique reduces defensiveness in others because it enables you to check the accuracy of your assumptions.

Perception checking is a four-step process:

Step 1: Describe the behavior (action) that you observed.

Step 2: Give one possible nonjudgmental reason (interpretation) for the behavior that you observed. (Possible reason 1)

Step 3: Give another *very different* possible reason for what happened. This should also be nonjudgmental. (Possible reason 2)

Step 4: Ask for a response.

Use a calm, pleasant tone of voice and direct eye contact. Negativity and sarcasm can block effective communication.

EXAMPLE

Step 1: "When you walked out of the office and left the door open," (Behavior description)

Step 2: were you in a hurry? (Reason 1)

Step 3: Or did you hurt yourself? (Reason 2)

Step 4: Or was something wrong? (Asking for a response)

TOOLS OF COMMUNICATION

Perception Checking

Instructions: Practice using the four-step perception-checking process. Compare your answers with a partner. This communication tool can also be used by a team working together to develop the responses.

EXERCISE 1

After you give the customer his order, he looks at you and frowns. What would you say?

1. Describe the behavior:

_____

_____

2. Interpretation (Reason) 1:

_____

_____

3. Interpretation (Reason) 2:

_____

_____

4. Ask for a response:

_____

_____

EXERCISE 2

When you ask the customer how she likes the repair work that you just finished, the customer sighs and says, "Well, it's O.K." What would you say?

1. Describe the behavior:

_____

_____

2. Interpretation (Reason) 1:

_____

_____

3. Interpretation (Reason) 2:

_____

_____

4. Ask for a response:

_____

_____

In addition to the direct questions and the rewording process discussed and practiced in Chapter 4, perception checking can be a useful communication tool for relating to customers on the telephone as well as in person.

6.3   COMMUNICATING WITH CUSTOMERS ON THE TELEPHONE

Talking to customers on the telephone and answering business calls courteously are essential to job success. There are effective ways to answer and make business calls. Remember the following points in order to be more effective:

- *Identify yourself* and the firm at once in a cheerful voice, for example, "Jones and Company, Joe Smith speaking." When answering for others, avoid abruptness. Don't say, "Who's calling?" It's more polite to ask, "May I tell her who's calling, please?" or "How may I help you?"

- *Give courteous attention* to callers' requests or complaints. Let the callers tell their own version of what happened in their own way instead of hurrying them or trying to tell them what they want.

- *Be tactful, avoid asking needless questions, and use the customer's name* whenever possible. For example, "Joe, I'm sorry the part didn't get here when we promised. Will next week work for you?"

- *Always remember to keep your promise* if you agree to call back. A broken promise can mean an angry customer.

- *Record the complete information neatly,* including the time and date of the call. Be sure to check for accuracy.

- Give the caller a choice of waiting or having a return call if you can't answer the caller's concern immediately. Customers will appreciate concern for their time. If the caller is placed on hold, return every 30 to 60 seconds to ask if the caller wants to continue to hold.

- If you become very busy and cannot handle all the calls, try a request such as: *"Thank you for calling us. We really want to serve you, but right now we are very busy. Will you please call back in 20 minutes so we will be able to help you more efficiently?"* or *"Thank you for calling. We are very busy right now. Please leave your number and we will return your call within the next hour."*

- *Express appreciation* for all calls, and close them courteously.

To communicate with angry, complaining, or talkative callers, use the following tips:

- If the person is angry, make notes and tell the caller you are doing this. When you make notes, callers know you are interested enough to write down their complaints.

- Summarize and reword what the person has said. This will tell the caller you do understand his or her position, needs, and frustrations.

- When calling someone who will talk too long if allowed, start the conversation with: "Good morning, Mary. I have three questions for you."

- If a call seems as if it won't end, inject "Just one more thing before we hang up . . ."

When initiating a call to another company as a representative of your company:

- Identify yourself and your company's name quickly. Next, give the name of the contact person you are trying to reach.
- State the reason for calling briefly and directly.
- Before placing telephone orders, write out all specifications to avoid confusion or delay.
- If the purpose of the call is to make a complaint, explain the problem calmly and courteously. You will receive better attention by avoiding accusations, irritation, and impatience.
- Conclude all business calls pleasantly and promptly by thanking the contact person.

(Association and Society Manager)

TOOLS OF COMMUNICATION

Customers and the Telephone

Instructions: Working in a group of three people, plan a realistic telephone response to an angry customer who calls to complain about a job that is late. One person should play the role of the customer, the second answers the customer, and the third person audiotapes the responses and plays them back. Take turns until you have all played each role and evaluate one another's answers.

- Which responses are the most effective?
- Which responses are the least effective?
- What could be done to improve the telephone techniques?

6.4 RESPONDING TO CRITICAL CUSTOMERS

WORLD OF WORK   Good service has always been the main reason for customers to bring return business. One supervisor said the cost of finding a new customer is five times greater than the cost of keeping a present customer happy. However, an unhappy customer will tell 8 to 10 people about a bad experience with a company.

Customers need to know your business cares about their needs. When an angry or critical customer telephones or comes to talk to you in person, give him or her your undivided attention.

In the beginning, just listen to angry customers. Let them vent. Do not interrupt or try to explain. Then:

1. Get more details.
   a. Get specific information through:
      - Summarizing
      - Asking direct questions such as:
         - What do you want me to do on this project?
         - When did you expect the job to be done?

   b. You may even need to guess about what is wrong—for example: "Is it our service you are unhappy with?"

   c. Ask what the customer wants—for example: "Do you want us to redo the work or refund your money?"

   d. Ask if anything else is wrong—for example: "Are there any other problems with the repairs we made?"

2. Agree with the customer.

   a. Acknowledge the truth of what he or she says—for example: "I understand you expected this job would be finished this week."

   b. Acknowledge his or her opinion—for example: "I realize you thought your job would cost less than this amount."

3. Suggest a solution—for example: "May we loan you a substitute until yours is ready?"

4. End on a positive note. You may not always win over all the customers to your opinion, but at least thank them for bringing the problem to your attention.

All of these responses will not be used at the same time or with *every* angry customer. Use only those responses most appropriate to the current situation.

TOOLS OF COMMUNICATION

How to Relate to Critical Customers

Instructions: Work with a partner to develop responses to the following criticism. Use the process outlined above. Share your solutions with the class. The class can discuss and vote on the two best problem-solving teams. If you are working alone, discuss the situation with a friend and ask him or her to work with you on this project.

Customer: "You told me this job would be reasonable, and now you say it will cost $294. No way is that price reasonable. I thought this was an honest shop! What's more, that's not the color you told me it would be. You said it would be brown, but this color is almost black."

_____

_____

_____

_____

_____

6.5 UNDERSTANDING CULTURAL DIFFERENCES

When dealing with customers from other cultures it is very important to be aware of cultural differences. Cultural variations in business customs can occur in organizations, in different parts of the city, and in various geographic regions of this nation, as well as globally. Some cultural differences appear when:

- People from two different age groups start to communicate, and differing value systems emerge. One may desire quality products and the other prefer quantity production.

- One person is more interested in direct communication while conducting business, but the other person wants to establish a relationship prior to getting down to the details of a business transaction.

- Someone wants to talk in generalities about the issues involved in creating designs, planning work, vacation schedules, and the like, and the second person wants to elaborate on the specific details.

- An employer, employee, or customer insists on jumping ahead of the chain of command rather than trying to solve a problem at the immediate level. Some will view this "I want to see the boss" attitude as a power play.

- Personal and family needs are given higher priorities than commitment to the work or the company.

- A new employee is expected to accomplish a task but is given no directions about *how* to do it.

WORLD OF WORK

An American employee who was working in Argentina quit a job that paid well because he could not adjust to the Argentine style of socializing with business prospects before *any* decisions about orders were made. His preference was to make the business dealing a top priority instead of waiting to get to know the people prior to business transactions.

When a person communicates across cultures, sometimes it is necessary to begin business discussions with seemingly trivial topics to establish some personal relationship before others are ready to talk about the work that needs to be done. Such a conversation could start with questions like these:

"How was your flight?"

"How's your family?"

"What's the weather like at this time of year where you come from?"

"What do you like to do in your free time?"

Understanding and valuing differences is essential to the success of both customer sales and service. Success is more likely to occur if you take time to research the values of other cultures when relating to people from other parts of the world or even in different areas of the United States.

If workers do not learn to adjust to personal and cultural differences, then issues of *harassment* may arise, which may lead to lawsuits.

Harassment was defined by multicultural specialist Denise Osei (1995) as "Any type of behavior that causes an employee or customer to feel uncomfortable. This could be classified as repeated offending behavior or a significant one-time attack, either verbal or nonverbal." Harassment by coworkers or leaders is often the cause of costly lawsuits, large cash settlements to victims, or the dismissal of the offender. *Any* type of harassment creates a negative work environment. Note the real-life situations reported in the case studies included in this chapter. Unfortunately, these examples are typical of work situations where people have differing value systems.

Stress Less

Before going home, allow yourself time to relax so that you can deal with what is happening on the home front in a relaxed manner. To accomplish this, try the following stress-relief technique. Sit in your car or on a bench in a waiting area, close your eyes, and breathe deeply for five minutes.

6.6 APPLYING THE CONCEPTS

CASE STUDY

Joe continually complains that you are slacking off and not producing as much work as the rest of the team. Joe also says your work is not of good quality and your coffee breaks are too long. He has made these comments repeatedly in front of everyone in the break room.

Work with a partner to decide how you would handle this situation if you were the person being harassed.

CASE STUDY

Imagine you are the supervisor, and observe the following situation as it develops.

A customer with an accent walks up to buy some supplies and your employee at the counter keeps asking the customer to repeat what he wants. Finally, the customer gets what he needs and starts to leave. The employee turns to a coworker and says in a rather loud voice, "If these people are going to live here, why don't they learn to speak English so you can understand them?"

How would you handle the immediate situation with the customer? How would you follow up this situation with the employee(s)?

CHAPTER PROJECT

Use the format below to prepare an outline for a sales, service, or technical presentation. Make sure it includes at least two of the five basic human needs listed in this chapter. Work in a team of three to five members. Select the type of presentation you will prepare, either for listeners with no knowledge of your career or listeners who are experts in your field. Give a 15- to 20-minute group presentation to the class. If possible, videotape the class presentation for more accurate self-evaluation. Feedback from other students and the instructor is very useful in assessing the strengths and weaknesses of the presentation.

Organizing your ideas will help you to remember the main points. When talking with any group, use two to five main ideas with supporting details, including logical and emotional support. A well-thought-out organization makes it much easier for listeners to enjoy hearing your ideas.

VERBAL PRESENTATION GUIDELINES

I. The general purpose of the report is:

    A. To give—within a certain time frame—the facts, figures, and information necessary for the listeners to understand the subject you are presenting.

    B. To present the information in an interesting style.

II. The specific purpose of this assignment is:

    A. To give you an opportunity to present subject matter for either one of the two different types of listeners. (Choose 1 or 2.)

        1. For listeners who have no knowledge of the field. The listeners may include business people, students, or politicians.

        2. For a group of experts from your particular field or specialists from your general area of business or industry.

    B. To know as much as possible about the audience so you can adjust your presentation to their knowledge.

III. Make your presentation interesting and energetic.

    A. Both untrained and trained people are human beings; they react favorably to talks that are vital and dynamic.

        1. The material should be well organized and carefully thought out so that it will have real value.

        2. The presentation should be effective, conversational, and detailed.

        3. Communicate with energy and enthusiasm, and make direct eye contact when speaking to the listeners.

    B. The introduction and the conclusion are very important to a presentation for either type of audience.

    C. Use visual aids to add to the understanding of the information.

    D. Use verbal supports to help the audience understand each major idea that is presented, and because ideas must be carefully supported with proof. These may include:

        1. Definitions

        2. Facts

        3. Statistics

        4. Examples

        5. Quotations

            a. From experts

            b. From customers

        6. Comparisons with other products

IV. Prepare an outline for the report. Designate who is responsible for which part of the presentation.

    A. See the outline template below. Every speech must include the following to be complete:

        1. Title of the presentation

        2. Introduction

        3. Body

        4. Conclusion

          5. Works cited (listing any information from outside sources)

            a. Printed information

            b. Individuals interviewed

               (1) Name, position, and company

               (2) Place, city, and state

               (3) Date and time

    B. Give the outline to the instructor at the time of the presentation.

  V. Use note cards to speak.

  VI. Use visual aids to illustrate statistics and quotations for greater impact.

    A. Check the print to see if it is large enough to be seen by every person in the room.

    B. Flip charts, posters, transparencies, and PowerPoint aids should have a maximum of five lines per page or slide. Be sure the print contrasts distinctly with the background for ease of reading.

  VII. To make this presentation as professional as possible, consider wearing business-type clothing.

    A. For a man, it is appropriate to wear a shirt, a tie, and a sweater or sports jacket.

    B. For a woman, choose a simple dress, a suit, or nice slacks and a jacket.

    C. For a shop presentation, wear clothing suitable for the situation.

  VIII. Convey enthusiasm about your ideas, and the presentation will be outstanding.

OUTLINE TEMPLATE

Title _____

Introduction

    Create interest   I. _____

                   A. _____

                   B. _____

    Specific purpose II. _____

    (thesis statement) _____

Body

    First main idea   I. _____

    Supporting details A. _____

                   B. _____

    Second main idea II. _____

                   A. _____

                   B. _____

Conclusion

    Summarize   I. _____

    Encourage action II. _____

PRESENTATION EVALUATION FORM

Class members and the instructor can use this evaluation form to provide feedback for the presentation individual team members.

Speaker:

Evaluator:

Title: Date:

	POOR	FAIR	GOOD	EXCELLENT
CONTENT:				
Introduction:	▣	▣	▢	☐
Gained attention	▣	▣	▢	☐
Made purpose clear	▣	▣	▢	☐
Body of speech:	▣	▣	▢	☐
Well organized	▣	▣	▢	☐
Interesting ideas with supporting details	▣	▣	▢	☐
Emotional	▣	▣	▢	☐
Logical supports	▣	▣	▢	☐
Conclusion:	▣	▣	▢	☐
Summary	▣	▣	▢	☐
Created lasting impression	▣	▣	▢	☐
DELIVERY:				
Confidence, enthusiasm:	▣	▣	▢	☐
Voice:	▣	▣	▢	☐
Loud enough	▣	▣	▢	☐
Interesting	▣	▣	▢	☐
Body action:	▣	▣	▢	☐
Posture	▣	▣	▢	☐
Gestures	▣	▣	▢	☐
Eye contact:	▣	▣	▢	☐
Overall impression of speech:	▣	▣	▢	☐

Comments:

DISCUSSION QUESTIONS

1. Do you agree with the concept that coworkers should be classified as internal customers? Why or why not?
2. Do you believe coworkers should be given greater consideration by the employer than external customers? Why or why not?
3. Would your ranking of basic human needs be the same as Maslow's? If not, where would you differ?
4. What are some cultural differences you have noticed between individuals?

SUMMARY

In this chapter, you had the opportunity to use some communication tools essential to communicating successfully with customers and coworkers. These tools were:

- Learning names quickly
- Using the telephone effectively
- Checking perception accurately
- Responding to criticism productively
- Understanding and relating to cultural differences
- Making an oral team presentation

If you believe you are proficient in using these communication tools, then you are ready to move to the next chapter, on working in teams. If you cannot apply them automatically, now would be a good time to review this chapter and practice using the skills until you feel confident.

CHAPTER 7

Teamwork: Communicating Productively with Coworkers

LEARNING OBJECTIVES

1. Discover trends in the workplace of the future.

2. Learn about creating a positive communication climate with coworkers.

3. Learn about and practice communicating without hostility.

4. Learn and practice giving and receiving instructions productively.

5. Analyze leadership styles.

6. Learn to give orders effectively.

7. Learn to solve problems creatively.

8. Apply the concepts.

Industrial relations managers, personnel directors, and supervisors from every type of business and industry in all parts of the United States have declared that communication tools are important—often critical—to success on the job. These forward-looking employers often refer to their employees as **internal** customers because they are as valuable to the company as the more traditional **external** customer.

When you think about yourself working for the company of your choice—a plant, a shop, a hospital, or a computer center—what do you think about? Do you visualize yourself utilizing the skills you are learning in your field, such as building new equipment or using the latest technology to maintain it?

Undoubtedly, you see yourself succeeding with the abilities necessary for advancing on the job. But do you see yourself with more than just the essential

169

skills? Do you see yourself communicating effectively with other employees? A successful employee is the man or woman who works well with others and communicates effectively, not only with external customers, but also with coworkers, the internal customers. This chapter will focus on the tools needed to communicate productively as a team member or team leader in the workplace of the future.

WORLD OF WORK

Richard Rock, an executive at eBay, which employs more than 1,200 workers, expressed concern about finding enough good employees. He said, "Critical thinking, problem solving and communication skills aren't really as abundant as you'd hope." He made this observation when he was in the process of donating money for high schools and higher education to encourage educators to let students know how their "lessons apply to their careers" (1999).

7.1 WHAT ARE OTHER TRENDS IN THE FUTURE?

What will be the nature of the workplace of the future? The former vice-president of marketing and public relations at Avista Utilities, Joanne Mathison (1995), discussed this future workplace and the skills and abilities employees will need to be successful. She stated that the forces of change are:

- Increasing competition
- Advancing technology
- Environmental issues
- Additional customer demands

This workplace will probably have just one supervisor for 50 people, with fewer management positions. In addition, employee and supervisor roles are changing.

Ms. Mathison stressed the changing employment contract. These differences in the work agreement can be described as:

- Management that is changing from a paternalistic attitude ("We'll take care of you") to empowering employees with the attitude "We'll help you take care of yourselves."
- Employees who will create job security for themselves through learning to become more "employable" by developing a variety of skills in order to be part of work teams, no matter what the future brings.
- Disappearance of clear career paths because employers need workers who can learn to adapt to rapidly changing technology, often for short periods of time.
- Employment relationships that are ceasing to be long term, with more temporary employees contracted outside of the company. These "temps" are working for many different companies in a lifetime.

Because of these changes, self-managed work teams are becoming more common. Employees are taking on more responsibility and more of the traditional supervisor's role. In addition, employees more frequently work to resolve their own conflicts. Another important aspect of these self-managed teams will be the need for employees to be multiskilled and able to function in various roles.

Future employees will work together to solve problems and train others. Self-managed groups have different team structures. These vary in the length of time they work together to accomplish a goal or complete a task, as well as the amount of control and authority the team possesses.

Short-term task force teams usually have a single focus, such as improving work schedules or planning a design for a special project. Groups with longer time commitments often work together in preparing quality products for customers. In this situation the team is often responsible for the entire process from the beginning to the end (Mathison, 1995).

WORLD OF WORK

A local trailer manufacturing company assigns its employees to teams. Each team is entirely responsible for the production, quality, and the time spent in the completion of one specific type of trailer.

Most employers desire the following teamwork skills in their employees:

- Efficient listening
- Effective feedback
- Productive communication with external customers and coworkers
- Explicit instructions, both when giving and receiving them
- Creative problem solving
- The ability to issue orders and requests in a positive way

WORLD OF WORK

During a team-building seminar, the director of materials for Sacred Heart Medical Center, Bruce Currer (1996), presented convincing evidence of the effectiveness of work teams. He stated that in the last year their printing services department had been able to increase output by 20 percent and reduce jobs printed late by 40 percent. This was accomplished with no additional staffing through the implementation of work teams.

Based on information from employers and data from the previous employer surveys, this chapter will concentrate on ways you can communicate in order to utilize each person's strengths and differences efficiently. One of the most helpful analyses of information has to do with the awareness and understanding of individual styles of communication, presented in Chapter 1. This understanding can aid in building a positive communication climate in the workplace.

7.2 BUILDING A POSITIVE COMMUNICATION CLIMATE

It is often difficult to achieve efficient communication, but if you understand the benefits of good communication, you will want to develop the communication skills that can be valuable to the ongoing maintenance of work teams. To develop strong job relationships by communicating in teams, start with the following techniques:

1. *Choose the correct time and place* for sharing ideas with your team. Rush hour is not a good time to discuss a creative solution to a problem or a change in work schedules.

2. *Speak with a definite goal in mind.* Do not just start to talk hoping that something significant will come out of your mouth.

■ Think before speaking.

■ Plan what you will say.

3. *Respect the dignity of others when you are speaking.*

■ Speak with honesty, but be aware of the feelings, needs, and interests of others.

■ Remember, it is constructive to question an idea, but it is destructive to attack a human being: (See the communication techniques described under "Communication without Hostility" below.)

■ If suggestions your leader makes are unacceptable, discuss them privately with the leader. Don't say, "That was a stupid idea." Instead, focus on the work. Then ask a question, for example, "What did you want to accomplish with the changes in production?"

4. *Change a negative communication to positive communication.* If someone speaks to you angrily, your natural inclination will be to reply with anger. Instead, strive for positive communication by avoiding sarcasm, expressions of boredom, or any other form of negative communication that puts others on the defensive.

5. *Listen objectively.* Realize that you, too, have prejudices and attitudes that can keep you from having an open mind about what is being said.

■ Understand that you may interpret a message incorrectly. People often hear only what they expect to hear, not what is actually said.

■ Practice rewording and summarizing as discussed in Chapter 4 or use perception checking as described in Chapter 6.

6. *Avoid withdrawing or becoming hostile.* These reactions only close the door to understanding.

7. *Understand that we all are different* because of our various experiences in life. When you respect differences, others will appreciate your understanding. Remember that those with alternative methods for accomplishing tasks are not deficient workers simply because their methods are different from yours.

8. *Strive to build trust.* Trust comes when there is acceptance of others. This does not mean that you will always agree with others, but it does allow honesty and openness.

9. *Verify the degrees of your success* while communicating.

■ Ask questions, and observe the listener's response, both verbally and nonverbally.

■ Reword statements. For example, when someone says "I'll be finished soon," respond with, "Do you mean five minutes or 30 minutes?"

■ Search for correct answers.

Because every human being has the right to courteous communication, it is essential to treat coworkers with the same respect that you would give external customers. Respecting coworkers, your "internal customers," also involves the communication skills discussed in Chapter 6:

1. Learn their names, by using some of the name-remembering techniques.

2. Recognize that coworkers, the *internal* customers, have the same basic human needs as the *external* customers.

3. Strive to understand those who are culturally diverse.

These techniques for building a positive communication climate can help you maintain a productive work environment. A negative workplace environment lowers employee morale and reduces productivity.

What are some factors that create positive or negative work environments?

TABLE 7.1	*Building a productive workplace.*
Communication Tools for a Productive Workplace	**Factors that Contribute to Unproductive Working Conditions**
Words like "please" and "thank you" are used to show respect for others.	Commands such as "Come here immediately!" or "Repair this now!" are used constantly.
Criticism or correction is given privately.	Criticism of workers is given in front of the rest of the team.
Disagreements with the supervisor are discussed privately with that person.	Workers make fun of a supervisor when he or she is not present.
Schedules are discussed with the appropriate person rather than complaining to those who have no control over them.	Workers complain or whine about work schedules and vacation times continually and have a "That's not fair!" attitude.

WORLD OF WORK

"Everybody likes to be noticed. But too often we toil in obscurity," asserts L. M. Sixel (1997) in the *Houston Chronicle*. He goes on to point out: "Bosses just don't give enough compliments. Some don't ever say a nice word about a nice job; others may give an occasional pat on the back, but it rings hollow. Praise may sound like a fuzzy feel-good topic—smacking of a group hug in the middle of a meeting—but compliments are an important motivator at work. Done well, they stimulate more good work. But if they're done poorly—or not at all—it depresses morale."

7.3 COMMUNICATION WITHOUT HOSTILITY

No matter how hard you try, sometimes positive communication climates just do not develop, and a negative, damaging, hostile climate takes over. In this kind of climate, *defensive communication* is common. We use defensive communication when we feel under attack by another person so we put on a protective armor to avoid being hurt. Our "armor" is often composed of a counterattack on the critic, sarcasm, withdrawing, apathy, or going home to yell at the dog.

If more constructive communication methods are used, conflict often can be avoided or at least controlled to develop an open atmosphere between customers and among team members.

Describe the problem rather than evaluate it. Say, "This is late," not "You're too slow." Instead of, "You are so disorganized, that's why we have to stay late," try "I get frustrated when we have to stay overtime and I have scheduled other things."

Be problem-oriented rather than trying to control problems. When a conflict occurs within a team, try to get each member's opinion about a solution. "This is what I want, so do it!" is not a problem-oriented statement. Instead, ask each person, preferably during a group meeting, but at least individually, "What can be done to solve this problem?" Then ask the group to evaluate and help choose and implement the best ideas.

Demonstrate concern for your team. For example, if someone says, "I'm late because my child is sick," and the team leader responds, "That's a personal problem, and I don't want to hear about it," the employee may feel devalued. Devalued employees usually do not develop strong company loyalty or energetic work habits. Instead, when someone on the team tells you he or she is late because of a sick child, you might try saying, "It is difficult to try and balance the needs of your family with the demands here at work." This reflects a caring attitude.

Avoid generalizations. Instead of "You are *always* late," or "You *never* do anything right," say "I was frustrated when this job was late."

Treat others as equals. You can create an open atmosphere by avoiding putting yourself ahead of others. For example, instead of the team leader planning all the work schedules, ask for input in the planning process.*

Not all five techniques will be applied in every situation, but using at least one or two of these methods can reduce defensiveness in problem situations.

* These methods are adapted from Jack Gibbs, as quoted in Adler and Towne (1993), pp. 379–384.

TOOLS OF COMMUNICATION

Communication Without Hostility

Instructions: Working in pairs, develop responses to the following situations using the communication techniques above. When you are done, share your solutions with the class and decide which are the most productive uses of these methods.

Situation 1: A long-time customer comes to you and demands your immediate attention.

Describe the problem, don't evaluate.

_____

Ask the customer to suggest a solution.

_____

Ask the customer's concerns.

_____

Stay focused on the problem at hand, and avoid generalizations.

_____

Treat the customer as an equal.

_____

Situation 2: A new employee wants you to explain how to accomplish some repair work and you are very busy.

Describe the problem, don't evaluate.

_____

Ask the employee to suggest a solution.

_____

Ask the employee's concerns.

_____

Stay focused on the problem at hand, and avoid generalizations.

_____

Treat the employee as an equal.

_____

Using positive communication techniques also helps when giving and receiving instructions.

7.4   GIVING INSTRUCTIONS

We give and receive instructions almost daily about how to follow a procedure or use a new product, in both our personal and our professional lives. Instructions are frequently given and received in a haphazard manner, rather than being concise and organized. Knowing how to give instructions effectively will save time and money.

WORLD OF WORK

Bonneville Power in Washington state *requires* employees to know how to instruct other employees in the various methods the company uses.

When *giving* instructions, the goal is to have your meaning understood. When *receiving* instructions we often assume we understood what was meant. Instead, the receiver must accept responsibility for understanding the instructions.

When giving instructions, it is important to remember these points:

- Get the attention of learners before beginning to give instructions. Establish rapport. Be friendly.
- State the desired objective, the goal, or the overall picture.

- Motivate the people to carry out your directions by letting them know the benefits of following your directions. For instance, they will be able to save time or money, or create a safer environment.

- Know the learner's level of technical vocabulary; relate to them in terms of their experience. Obviously, you would not use technical computer terminology to give instructions to someone who is unfamiliar with a keyboard or an icon.

- Give instructions in a logical sequence: "First, do this. Then second . . ." Use concise, clear language.

- Establish a system of orientation. You might use a clock face ("three o'clock," "six o'clock"); a map (north, south); or up–down, right–left.

- Give enough information to clarify but not to confuse. Information overload can cause some people to quit listening.

- Use positive communication to overcome language, physical, emotional, and listening barriers.

- Practice giving your instructions out loud.

- Seek feedback frequently as you give instructions. When you ask for feedback, do not ask, "Do you understand?" Instead, always phrase your questions so that you will know specifically what is understood. Ask the person to demonstrate how to follow your instructions in short steps and to tell you about each step using his or her own words.

- Give praise when the instructees complete the new actions correctly. If correction is necessary, give it constructively.

When giving instructions on the job, follow-up is essential because you need to know that your instructions are being carried out correctly.

TOOLS OF COMMUNICATION

Giving Instructions

Instructions:

1. Work in pairs.

2. Decide on a familiar task, tool, piece of equipment, instrument, game, or sport to use to give instructions to your partner. Practice using visual aids, and time yourself. Do not let your partner know what you will be doing ahead of time so that you can make the instructions more realistic.

3. Plan the instructions to last a total of seven to nine minutes, including feedback from the person you are instructing. This means you probably will be able to deal with only some limited aspect of the total process.

4. Explain to your partner the setting and purpose for the instructions. Where would the instructions be given? What time of day would you be giving your instructions? Time of day greatly influences the way it is necessary to communicate. (The last thirty minutes of the day are not an ideal time to give instructions!) Would any other people be involved? It is always important to include the motivation for learning. Be enthusiastic—let the person know *why* the process is necessary, including the *when, where,* and *how* of the process.

5. Give your instructions in a logical, step-by-step order. Give each step slowly enough to be understood. Explain any technical terms. Think of what the learner already knows and what else is needed for understanding. Finally, seek feedback to make certain the instructions are understood.

GIVING INSTRUCTIONS EVALUATION FORM

Evaluator's name :

Instructor: Subject:

Instructee: Date:

	POOR	FAIR	GOOD	EXCELLENT
1. **Set the scene**	☐	☐	☐	☐
a. Place and time	☐	☐	☐	☐
b. Individuals involved	☐	☐	☐	☐
2. **Gained attention of the person** before beginning	☐	☐	☐	☐
3. **Motivated the learner** by giving the reasons for instruction	☐	☐	☐	☐
4. **Gave goal or overall picture** of desired outcome	☐	☐	☐	☐
5. **Language used:**	☐	☐	☐	☐
a. Technical terms explained	☐	☐	☐	☐
b. Clear, precise words used	☐	☐	☐	☐
c. Avoided confusing details	☐	☐	☐	☐
6. **Logical step-by-step sequence**	☐	☐	☐	☐
a. Avoided backtracking	☐	☐	☐	☐
b. Order of ideas was meaningful to instructee	☐	☐	☐	☐
7. **Used visual aids to demonstrate instructions**	☐	☐	☐	☐
8. **Encouraged feedback from the learner:**	☐	☐	☐	☐
a. Asked for summary or rewording	☐	☐	☐	☐
b. Welcomed questions	☐	☐	☐	☐
c. Required feedback after short units of information	☐	☐	☐	☐
d. Allowed for a return to demonstration	☐	☐	☐	☐
9. **Gave learner encouragement and praise**	☐	☐	☐	☐
10. **Sounded enthusiastic and interested:**	☐	☐	☐	☐
a. Could be easily heard	☐	☐	☐	☐
b. Had variety in pitch and rate of speaking	☐	☐	☐	☐

7.5 LEADERSHIP STYLES

When you are in situations of leadership, are you a "let's get the job done and get out of here" type of leader, or are you the type of leader who wants to discuss the problem as a group and get everyone to agree to a solution before making a decision?

Every team needs a leader who is able to maintain focus on the project at hand. However, leaders who concentrate only on the job to be done may not be as efficient as they seem. They can miss valuable ideas and information because they do not consult all of the team members to evaluate or include their ideas.

Another reason for talking with other team members is that coworkers who contribute to the decision-making process will usually be more enthusiastic about the project when their ideas have been considered. When they are consulted, team members feel more valued as employees.

On the other hand, leaders who spend all their time talking about the task with team members and analyzing different approaches to the project can sometimes slow down production and miss important deadlines because they think one more bit of research or one more survey is needed. This type of leader may lose out because she or he suffers from the "paralysis of analysis" syndrome. If you are this type of leader, try to include some team members who will help you stay focused on the work that needs to be accomplished so your team can function more efficiently.

What is your personal style of leadership when working with a group? It is useful to assess your preferred method for leading a group to determine your personal team fit. When you have completed the following leadership analysis, ask two other people in the class, two close friends, or two coworkers if they have the same perception of you as a leader as you rated yourself. Color-code their responses on the leadership analysis form, and then write a thoughtful paragraph about your own perception of your leadership methods in comparison with others' analysis of your style.

WORLD OF WORK

An example of ineffective leadership occurred when a group of students were working together on a class project. Because they were so busy researching and analyzing the project, they failed to complete it on schedule and consequently received a low grade. A focus on analytical communication styles and people-oriented leadership styles afflicted this group with the "paralysis of analysis" syndrome.

TOOLS OF COMMUNICATION

Leadership Analysis

Instructions: The following factors suggest different preferences in leadership. Rate each factor according to whether you would act this way usually, often, rarely, or never. Then total the numbers for each column. Consider *all* experience—work, school, church (any time you have spent working with others).

	USUALLY	OFTEN	RARELY	NEVER
1. I usually act as the group leader or speaker.	☐	☐	☐	☐
2. When leading a group, I would encourage working overtime.	☐	☐	☐	☐
3. When leading a group, I prefer to let the team members create their own solutions to problems.	☐	☐	☐	☐
4. When leading a group, I prefer to settle problems by myself.	☐	☐	☐	☐
5. Sometimes I am buried in details.	☐	☐	☐	☐
6. I encourage competition between groups.	☐	☐	☐	☐
7. I prefer keeping the work going rapidly.	☐	☐	☐	☐
8. I believe the group leader should make the decisions about how, when, and what tasks need to be accomplished.	☐	☐	☐	☐
9. I can easily express my ideas in a group.	☐	☐	☐	☐
10. I believe team members should be encouraged to plan their own schedules.	☐	☐	☐	☐
11. I believe it is the responsibility of the team leader to assign the work.	☐	☐	☐	☐
12. I believe the team members should decide how fast work can be accomplished.	☐	☐	☐	☐
13. I believe it is not necessary for group leaders to explain their decisions to team members.	☐	☐	☐	☐
14. When leading the team, I would encourage the team to beat its previous record.	☐	☐	☐	☐
15. I believe more work can be accomplished when team members follow standard procedures.	☐	☐	☐	☐
TOTALS	☐	☐	☐	☐

Now go back and circle numbers 1, 3, 5, 9, 10, 12, and 15. If your highest score is in the **Usually** and **Often** columns for these numbers, then you are a more people-oriented team leader. Put a box around numbers 2, 4, 6, 7, 8, 11, 13, and 14. Add your score for these numbers in the **Usually** and **Often** columns. If these are higher, you are more task-oriented and would prefer focusing on the work that needs to be done rather than being concerned about the needs of the employees.

When you have the opportunity to be part of a self-managed work team, remember this analysis of your leadership preference. It will allow you to focus on your own strengths and make you aware of areas where you might be weak.

No matter what your preferred style of leadership is, remember to value each team member for his or her uniqueness and ability to contribute something of value to the team. Research has shown that productivity will increase and attitudes improve when employees are included in the decision-making process, because this creates a sense of worth and value in the employee. The team leader who maintains a balance between completing tasks efficiently and relating to coworkers effectively will maintain the highest team morale.

WORLD OF WORK

During a committee meeting, the members were discussing the strengths and weaknesses of potential job applicants. Some members of the interview committee insisted on repeating the same information again and again. The meeting was in its third hour when one member said, "Look, I know I'm a task-oriented person and most of you are not, but I need to go home. We've been over this information several times, it's two hours past quitting time, so let's make a decision we can all live with and leave." With that comment, they did return to the focus of the meeting, made a decision about hiring one of the applicants, and closed the meeting in fifteen minutes! This situation illustrates the need to have at least *one* task-oriented person on a committee.

7.6 GIVING ORDERS

Your role as a team leader will be more challenging and satisfying if you learn how to gain the cooperation of everyone on the team. Often it may be your job to **issue orders** to others. Learning to do so effectively will be a valuable communication skill throughout your career. Below are some points to keep in mind about giving orders.

- Orders are given in order to *regulate the contributions* of various members of the team—to keep them from working in opposition to the purposes of the team and to accomplish the goals of the organization.
- Orders are *not* a power trip or a way to make you feel good.
- The guiding principle must be: Give only those orders that are necessary.
- People will be quick to judge the manner in which orders are given and may react negatively or defensively if orders are issued inappropriately.

It will be to your benefit to learn various ways for giving orders to others. Even if you do not plan to be a team leader or supervisor, you may someday find yourself thrust into a leadership role. Learning effective methods for giving orders will be helpful during your career advancement. Orders may be given in one of four ways:

Request. The request form of an order is the most common form used by good team leaders and supervisors, and it will be wise to follow their example. You are probably already very familiar with several variations of the request, such as:

"As soon as you finish, Herb, will you please . . ."

"Sally, how about giving me a hand with . . ."

Most of what you set out to do may be accomplished by using the request method. It is a pleasant, easy way of asking other people to do something. This method works particularly well for people who, although they are excellent workers, must be treated carefully and not overused. It avoids irritating people or reminding them of the sometimes dictatorial methods of parents and teachers.

Suggestion. Often, an order can be given as an indirect suggestion. If you know your team members well, the hint will be more than sufficient. For example:

"We're supposed to get out 10 units today, Mike, and we're a little behind. Do you think we can make it up before quitting time?"

"Janet, are we doing everything we can to keep these records up to date?"

This type of order, like the request, will usually start the ball rolling. If others are responsible and like to feel they have been consulted about decisions, they will usually grasp the point of the suggestion immediately and take positive action to correct the situation. However, the suggestion is less effective with newer workers who do not have the background or experience to come up with sensible, practical solutions. Nor will the power of suggestion work with those who are undependable or incompetent.

Call for volunteers. Asking for voluntary assistance is a useful device in emergencies. Most people like the feeling of giving something extra to their jobs and often will want to help out in an unusual situation. Use this distress signal with great restraint. One of the standard jokes among employees concerns the supervisor who regards each project as a "special rush." In all likelihood, the team member who will hear and respond to the call for volunteers most frequently is a friend; yet, even this loyal person will draw the line if the appeal is made too often.

Command. Sometimes, the command order is the only way to get something done, but use it as a last resort and then probably only in an emergency. When this method is used, the team members will recognize it for what it is, because commands from parents and teachers have been a major experience in everyone's growing-up process. Because working adults tend to think they have left those commands behind, a direct command to one of your team members often is met with bitter antagonism. Such an emotional reaction is unfortunate, but the fact remains that emotions may take over and the meaning of the command will be lost. The only thing that will be clear to this person is that he or she is being ordered around.

As a team leader or supervisor, resign yourself to a simple fact: *The direct command is to be avoided whenever possible.* And on those rare occasions when you must use it, do so as calmly as possible.

Of course, the first thing to be sure of is that the most effective method of delivering orders has been chosen (request, suggestion, call for volunteers, or command). Then check to see if others have followed your orders to determine if the directions are clear. If the job is not being done correctly, or if there is a feeling of irritation from those working with you, you can be reasonably sure your ability to issue orders needs improvement.

TO MAKE YOUR ORDERS CLEAR

- Speak at an understandable rate of speech.
- Use a pleasant tone of voice.
- Assign work with a reasonable explanation of why, how, where, when, and what is supposed to happen.
- Check to see that each employee understands what she or he is told to do by asking for feedback.
- Be brief, direct, and to the point.
- Assign one job at a time whenever possible.
- Minimize your own importance.
- Use your own authority frankly rather than in the name of top management.
- Work through the chain of command instead of sidestepping it.
- Be impartial in distributing tasks.

This list can be used as a periodic review. Ask yourself whether you are accomplishing each item on the list. When you can answer "yes" to each one, you will be able to give orders effectively. As with any other skill, it takes practice to become proficient at giving orders successfully. Complete the following exercise to test your skill in giving orders.

TOOLS OF COMMUNICATION

Giving Orders

Instructions: Complete this assignment to develop expertise in the different styles of giving orders. Do this individually. When you have finished, work with four or five others and choose the most effective method and wording for each situation.

Assume you are the team leader. Circle the best method to use in each situation (request, suggestion, call for volunteers, or command). Then write the exact words you would use.

1. A customer is on the telephone requesting some technical information about the Super-Clipper, a computer sold by your firm. On your team, Jim Clementi is best qualified to give the information. Ask him to take the phone call.

Method used: Request   Suggestion   Call for volunteers   Command

Exact words: _____

_____

2. Your team is falling behind in its production schedule. The supervisor, Sandra, has specifically asked you to complete nine units today. You are the team leader, it is noon, and only three units have been finished. Give one type of order to speed things up.

Method used: Request   Suggestion   Call for volunteers   Command

Exact words: _____

_____

3. You see smoke coming from a corner of the warehouse. Be specific about how to handle the situation.

Method used: *Request*   *Suggestion*   *Call for volunteers*   *Command*

Exact words: _____

_____

4. You need the help of your assistant, Jane, to prepare a statistical report, but she is working on a project of her own.

Method used: *Request*   *Suggestion*   *Call for volunteers*   *Command*

Exact words: _____

_____

5. Henry Hanson's reports are especially messy and hard to read, and you want him to be neater.

Method used: *Request*   *Suggestion*   *Call for volunteers*   *Command*

Exact words: _____

_____

6. Phil and May are concerned about doing anything that is not in their job description. Today there is an urgent need for help with some heavy work in the plant, which will take about an hour. This work is not listed among their duties.

Method used: *Request*   *Suggestion*   *Call for volunteers*   *Command*

Exact words: _____

_____

7. The normal lunch hour schedule must be altered today because most of the team will be attending a special anniversary lunch. Unfortunately, one person on the team will have to stay at the office as troubleshooter until the lunch is over at about 2:00. Give someone this assignment.

Method used: *Request*   *Suggestion*   *Call for volunteers*   *Command*

Exact words: _____

_____

8. Describe a situation involving the need to give orders in a difficult situation:

Method used: *Request*   *Suggestion*   *Call for volunteers*   *Command*

Exact words: _____

_____

7.7   SYNERGY

What is **synergy?** Is it a contagious disease?

No! It's the energy formed by people who work in groups!

Depending on the group, this energy can be either negative or positive. Positive energy is generated when group members work together and increase one another's effectiveness. When group members fail to cooperate or display hostile attitudes, negative energy is produced.

WORLD OF WORK

Effective small-group communication had a significant importance to 94.2% of the 329 employers surveyed in the year 2000 (Clark, 2000).

Working in groups to find solutions to problems or to manage conflict can create a positive, energy-producing environment. The six-step problem-solving method below is an effective technique for generating positive energy. This creative problem-solving sequence was developed as a discussion procedure for applying research findings about human creativity. It is based on the work of Alex Osborn, Sidney J. Parnes, and others associated with the Creative Problem Solving Institute. The pattern is most fittingly applied to problems for which there are many possible solutions, such as how to improve some product, alternative uses for idle buildings or tools, or any situation needing imaginative solutions. This method can also be used when dealing with conflict in the workplace.

PROBLEM-SOLVING STEPS: THE CREATIVE METHOD

1. Analyze and define the problem by asking some of the following questions in your group:

    - What is the specific problem? What are the issues? Is money an issue? Use of time? Are there differences in facts, values, power, or ego?

    - Who is involved? Those in the shop, people in the office, or the president of the company?

    - How many are affected? The entire company or just a few teams?

    - What is the extent of the problem? Our department, the office, the city or state?

    - How long has it existed? Is it a new development, or an old one that has re-emerged?

    - Any other pertinent questions.

2. Brainstorm *all* possible solutions and make no evaluations about the solutions. During this time do not allow the use of killer responses like "We tried that once," "It costs too much," or "It won't work."

3. Decide on criteria for evaluating brainstormed solutions. Will the decision be based on cost? Creativity? Time? Evaluate each possible solution.

4. As a group, decide on the best solution. Make sure that everyone agrees, not just a majority. Those who are not in favor of an idea can often create roadblocks, be unenthusiastic, and cause delays.

5. Now decide how the group will put the solution into effect.
   - Who will be involved? Will everyone in this group be included, or will two or three people gather information and report back to the entire group?
   - How many should be informed? In person? With e-mail or written memos? All the company or just those in the department?
   - Are other groups involved?
   - What is the time period for planning—a week, a month, a year, or ongoing?
   - What is the schedule for putting the solution into effect? When will you start and end the project, or is it indefinite?

6. Plan for follow-up.
   - Who will check the effectiveness of the solution?
   - What is the time frame for follow-up? When will evaluation reports take place?
   - What should happen if the solution is not effective?

To understand how this method can help you solve problems and make decisions, it will be useful to practice this process.

TOOLS OF COMMUNICATION

Problem-Solving Issues—Part I

Instructions: Divide the class into teams of four or five people. Each group will choose one of the following situations. Then, using the six-step problem-solving format, work to find a solution you would recommend to the team leader. Compare your solutions with those of other teams.

If you are working alone, assume you are the team leader and must deal with one of the following situations. Follow the six-step format and write out your ideas for each step.

1. An employee is not performing a required routine procedure. As the supervisor, you ask about it. The person says the procedure is unnecessary and the job is going well without it. How would you motivate this employee?

2. You have developed a new system of work procedures that will provide substantial savings in both time and money. However, adopting the system will require your team to make major changes in their daily routines. What would be a good way to get their cooperation?

3. Your staff has completed an assignment exactly as you had asked that it be done. Now you discover that your instructions were wrong, and the job should have been done another way. How would you approach the members of your team in this situation?

4. A team member comes to you obviously very upset with a grievance against the company. After hearing the story, you realize that much of the problem is the employee's fault. As the team leader, how would you respond to this person?

Problem-Solving Format—Part II

Instructions: Choose one of the preceding situations and, as a team, develop solutions.

1. Analyze the problem. What are the issues?

_____

_____

2. Brainstorm all possible solutions. Remember, no idea is too wild.

_____

_____

3. Decide on the criteria of evaluation (e.g., time, money, creativity), and evaluate each brainstormed idea.

_____

_____

4. As a team, choose the best solution.

_____

_____

5. Decide how you will implement your team's chosen solution (who will do what and when).

_____

_____

6. How and when will you know if your solution is working? What are the team's plans for follow-up?

_____

_____

In addition to these work situations, many other issues affect communication with coworkers, customers, and employers. Continue to use this method until your problem-solving skills become automatic.

WORLD OF WORK

"When I interview prospective employees, I am much more interested in their ability to work with others than their grade point average."—Supervisor, Agilent Company, Spokane Division

Stress Less

If you are the team leader, you may be causing stress unintentionally within your team by giving vague instructions, arranging rigid work schedules, or failing to recognize work that is accomplished ahead of schedule. When you are in a position of leadership, you can reduce your coworkers' stress by:

- Giving specific instructions
- Developing flexible work schedules that allow team members time to meet family commitments and deal with emergencies
- Giving praise and recognition for those who have exceeded work expectations

CASE STUDY

A team leader has recently experienced the following situations with two different members of the team. Form classroom teams and, using the six-step problem-solving method, discuss how you would recommend that the leader handle these problems.

CASE 1

Joanna, a native of Brazil, tells you that Thomas keeps asking her to go out with him. He has done this at least three times a week since she started to work with his team six months ago. When she politely but firmly refuses him, he says things like, "I know all you women from South America are party animals and stay out all night, so how come you won't go out with me? I can show you a good time." She goes on to say that he has also recently been brushing against her every time he walks by her work station. What would you recommend?

CASE 2

Joe has been working on your team for almost a year. During this time, Joe and Charlie have gotten to be good friends, so Joe thinks Charlie would not mind if he borrowed a splicer from his toolbox, since he left his at home and Charlie is not present to ask if he can borrow it. However, when Joe opens the toolbox he is very surprised to find some drugs—crack and some marijuana joints. Joe tells you, the team leader, about this situation. What are you going to do?

7.8 APPLYING THE CONCEPTS

CHAPTER PROJECT

This three-part project incorporates many of the communication tools presented in this chapter as well as previous chapters. Perception checking, verifying information, using positive nonverbal communication, problem solving in teams, persuading others by appealing to their basic needs and desires, researching companies, and contacting local businesses on the phone or in person can all be developed as you work through Parts A, B, and C of the final project. This project could also be of further assistance in building your network of employers if you consult them for accurate information about it.

Part A: Organizing Your Company

Instructions: Form teams with four or five members. Your team will be the members of your company. You will create a notebook recording your progress and decisions to be turned in for a grade.

1. Elect a team leader, president of the company, or chair of the board. The title will be the choice of the group. Someone will also need to be responsible for recording plans. In addition, you may need to set regular meeting dates outside of the allowed class time.

2. Use the six-step problem-solving method to brainstorm and decide on a product your company could produce or a service it could perform that would motivate others to invest in your company.

3. Assign or volunteer for areas of responsibility. These could include:

   - *Analyze the market:* What do people want or need? How many people would buy the product or use the service?

   - *Create advertisements:* Find out the cost of ads for radio, television, and newspapers. Be specific in designing ads.

   - *Establish a location:* What locations are available? What is the cost? What other companies would be in competition? Create a map to mark the business property you plan to use. A local commercial real estate agent or Web search might help with this aspect.

   - *Evaluate all expenses:* How much initial investment is needed for equipment, supplies, salaries, etc.? Contact other similar businesses, and explain the project. They usually are very cooperative in helping students to complete assignments of this nature. If some business person does give you an appointment, do not exceed the time set aside for you and be sure to send a thank-you letter following such a meeting.

Part B: Sales Presentation

Instructions: Once your company has made its decisions on Part A of this project, prepare a 20- to 25-minute group sales presentation for the class based on the sales outline in Chapter 6.

1. Decide how to motivate investors. Appeal to their needs and desires to be safe, save money, or have fun when they use your product or service.

2. Design sample ads for the investors to see or hear.

3. Illustrate the costs for the investors. Use charts, graphs, overhead transparencies, or handouts for the class investors to examine. It is usually ineffective to explain the expenses only verbally, because most people do not retain several numbers at a time when they are delivered only verbally. If you choose to use a poster, make sure the figures are large enough to be seen by those at the back of the room, not just those in front. A well-organized computer presentation using a program such as PowerPoint can be very persuasive.

4. If you want to sell a product, try to have a sample available for investors to see, taste, or smell.

5. Designate who will present which part.

6. Practice, practice, practice out loud. Time yourselves so that the group does not exceed the allotted period.

7. Be sure to include attention-getting opening and closing comments within the allowed time. There is nothing more boring than just announcing your product or service. Look at the difference between these two approaches:

   "I want to show you our new food product."

   vs.

   "Are you usually tired when you go home from work and need to fix a meal? What will it be, pizza again? How about something inexpensive, non-fattening, timesaving, and different? Our new food product, 'Super Suppers in a Bag,' can meet all of these needs for you!"

   Which approach appeals to you as being more effective? You should close your sales presentation with similar thought-provoking ideas.

8. Also, allow three or four minutes for questions and answers from the audience at the end of the group presentation. Someone from your group should also close the question and answer period by thanking the "investors" for their time and attention.

9. Audiences in the business world and in the classroom appreciate presentations that begin and end on time, so make every effort to stay within the time period.

10. Use the feedback forms at the end of Chapter 6 to evaluate one another's company presentations. The instructor will assign an evaluator for each person in the company and also will evaluate the presentations by the team leaders and team members.

Part C: Investment Time

Instructions: This will take place after all groups have finished their presentations and each company leader has given a two- or three-minute review of their product or service. Part C is not graded or evaluated, but it does help you to determine the effectiveness of your group's presentation.

1. Each student should bring replicas of two $5,000 stock certificates like the one that appears here.

2. After the presentations, select a company for an investment. Only one stock certificate can be invested in your *own* company. You *must* diversify and choose another company for your second $5,000 investment. When you make this decision, you will need to say why you think this other

---

STOCK CERTIFICATE

$5,000.00

_____
Name of Company or Product invested in

_____
Name of Investor

_____
Sign here

GUARANTEED & BONDED

company is a worthwhile investment as you give that company your $5,000 investment certificate.

3. The companies will then add up their investments, and the company with the most stock investors is the winner.

(Salisbury, 1989)

CRITERIA FOR FINAL PROJECT GROUP REPORT

Part A will be evaluated by the instructor using the following criteria:

1. How effectively the group functions as a team	40 points
2. Organization of the notebook	30 points
3. Creativity	10 points
4. Mechanics (spelling, sentence structure, punctuation)	20 points

Part B will be evaluated by the instructor. The instructor will award a maximum of 50 points for each participant. Class members will also provide feedback to the groups.

Part C will not be graded.

DISCUSSION QUESTIONS

1. Are you aware of any additional trends or new developments in the workplace that pertain to your career? If so, describe them.

2. What are the communication factors that create a positive work climate for you? What factors contribute to a negative climate?

3. Do you agree with the analysis of your leadership style? Why or why not? What type of leadership appeals to you? What do you think happens when a person's score for the "task orientation" style of leadership is very close to the "people orientation" style?

4. When giving orders at work, which type of order do you respond to most quickly? Do you agree that the "command" type of order should be used as little as possible? Why or why not?

SUMMARY

This chapter gave you the opportunity to do the following:

- Learn about trends in the workplace.
- Learn how to communicate without hostility.
- Give and understand productive instructions.
- Evaluate various leadership styles.
- Understand the process of giving effective orders.
- Work in creative problem-solving groups.

Understanding and using these processes will help you become more successful in your career.

References

Adler, Ronald B., & Towne, Neil. *Looking Out Looking In.* Fort Worth, TX: Harcourt Brace College Publishers, 1993.

Archibald, Jason. "Cover Letter Spacing Directions." Unpublished exercise, February 2001.

Association and Society Manager. Los Angeles: Barrington Publications.

Boggs, Alison. "Engine Shop Greases Workers' Palms." *The Spokesman Review,* Vol. 14, December 1996, p. A1.

Clark, Val. "Employers' Survey Results." 1983, 1992, 1998, 2000.

Clark, Val (Director). *Moving into Your Future, Part I.* Video cassette, Cottage Video and Spokane Community College, 1995.

Crandall, Steve. "Professionally Speaking; Building a Better Resume." *Microsoft Certified Professional Magazine,* March 2001, pp. 72–73.

Currer, Bruce. Lecture, Spokane Community College, February 1996.

Donlin, Kevin. "What to Do When Nothing Happens." www.CollegeRecruiter.com/1dayresumes.html. February 2001.

Employment Seminar. PBS/KSPS, Spokane, WA, February 11, 1996.

Guffey, Mary Ellen. *Business Communication News,* Spring 1995, p. 1.

Half, Robert. *USA Today,* July 18, 1989.

Hess, David. *Job Search.* Unpublished research, Aug. 2001.

Jacobs, Joanne. "$ Off Track." *The Spokesman Review,* February 25, 1996, p. B5.

Jardine, Douglas. "The Pressure to Change." *Pacific Northwest Leadership Connections,* Spring–Summer 1996, p. B5.

Jones, Daniel. "Hearing Is Not Necessarily Listening." *Rekindle/ISFI,* March 1998, pp. 17, 18.

Kennedy, Joyce, & Morrow, Thomas. "Electronic Resume Revolution." Quoted in *Business Communication News,* Spring 1995, p. 2.

Lamberton, Lowell, & Minor, Leslie. *Human Relations: Strategies for Success.* Chicago: Irwin Mirror Press, 1995.

Le Boeuf, Michael. *How to Win Customers and Keep Them for Life.* Berkeley: Berkeley Books, 1989.

Mathison, Joanne. "The Workplace of the Future." Conference presentation, 1995, Spokane, WA.

Miller, Leslie. "How Can You Develop an E-mail Friendly Resume?" Unpublished exercise, February 2001.

Morgan, David. "Resume Warning." Unpublished exercise, December 2000.

Nichols, R. A. "He Who Has Ears." Lecture audiotape, 1957.

Ober, Scott. *Contemporary Business Communication,* Fourth edition. Boston, MA: Houghton Mifflin Co., 2001, pp. 536–537.

Osei, Denise. *Moving into Your Future, Part I.* Video cassette, 1995.

Paetro, Maxine. "Mission Employable." *Mademoiselle,* June 2000, p. 66.

Power of Listening, The. Film. CRM/McGraw-Hill, 1984.

Roach, Lois. "Skills Assessment," "Paraphrasing," and "Oral Reports." Unpublished exercises.

Rock, Richard. "Ebay Executive Passing On His Lessons of Success." Quoted in *The Spokesman Review,* November 27, 1999, pp. A1 and 10.

Rosenbluth, Hal F., & Peters, Diane McFerrin. *The Customer Comes Second.* New York: William Morrow, 1992.

Salisbury, Linda Seppa. "Creating a Company." Unpublished exercises, 1989.

Sixel, L. M. "Jobs Should Offer Praise and Raises." Quoted in *The Spokesman Review,* December 30, 1997, p. D2.

Smith, Ken. "Online: Just When You Thought Your Resume Was Complete." *Hosteur,* Fall 1995, p. 18.

"Sorry I Wasn't Listening." *Compressed Air Magazine,* June 1998, pp. 20–24.

Sperry Univac. Listening Seminar, *Participants' Workbook,* 1983.

Stafford, Diane. "A Hire Calling." *The Spokesman Review,* August 27, 2000, p. D3.

"Stress." Cardiac Rehabilitation Center, Deaconess Medical Center, 1988, pp. 1–10.

U.S. Coordinating Council. *Job Finding Kit.*

Webster's New World Dictionary of the American Language, 2nd college ed. (Daniel B. Guraluik, editor-in-chief). New York: Simon & Schuster, 1986.

Index